WEATHER

AIR MASSES—CLOUDS—RAINFALL
STORMS—WEATHER MAPS—CLIMATE

by
PAUL E. LEHR
Meteorologist
National Oceanic and Atmospheric Administration

R. WILL BURNETT
Professor of Science Education Emeritus
University of Illinois

HERBERT S. ZIM

Illustrated by HARRY McNAUGHT

GOLDEN PRESS • NEW YORK
Western Publishing Company, Inc.
Racine, Wisconsin

FOREWORD

Of all aspects of the natural world, weather is outstanding in its beauty, its majesty, its terrors, and its continual direct effect on us all. Because weather involves massive movements of invisible air and is concerned with the temperature and pressure changes of this almost intangible substance, most of us have only a limited understanding of what weather is all about. This book will help you to understand it and also to understand, in some degree, how weather changes are predicted.

In the difficult attempt to portray the weather simply, accurately, and graphically we have had invaluable assistance from colleagues, experts, and many organizations. The National Weather Service helped us liberally with information and photos. Cloud photographs from pp. 16-20 were secured from Cloud Chart, Inc. Helpful material was supplied also by the Smithsonian Institution, the American Meteorological Society and its secretary, Kenneth F. Spengler, the National Safety Council, Dr. David M. Ludlam of the Franklin Institute, Lt. John H. Boone (USAF), and Lt. John F. Mann, Jr. ((USAF). Bernice Burnett and Adele F. Lehr read and criticized the manuscript at various stages. Dr. Vincent J. Schaefer of the Munitalp Foundation examined both text and illustrations and offered much helpful advice.

P.E.L.
R.W.B.
H.S.Z.

GOLDEN®, A GOLDEN GUIDE®, GOLDEN PRESS® and GOLDENCRAFT® are trademarks of Western Publishing Company, Inc.

CONTENTS

EVERYBODY TALKS ABOUT THE WEATHER Charles Dudley Warner said, "Everybody talks about the weather, but nobody does anything about it." Everyone, at times, feels as Warner did. The spoiled family picnic, the withered crops, all remind us how dependent we are on the weather. That is why weather is our most common topic of conversation, a factor in much of our agricultural, industrial, and civic planning, and a constant concern of everyone.

Warner was wrong. Something is being done. Today the science of weather—meteorology—is used to make our lives safer and better. Some types of forecasts are 95 per cent accurate. Storms are tracked and warnings are given. Clouds are being seeded to cause rainfall where it is needed. A network of weather stations enables planes to fly safely. A continued program of research reveals more and more about the weather. This introduction to weather will help you understand it.

Earth, to scale,
seen against the sun

What Makes the Weather?

Weather is the condition of the atmosphere in terms of heat, pressure, wind, and moisture. These are the elements of which the weather is made. Where the atmosphere thins to nothingness, there is no weather. There is no weather on the moon, for it has no atmosphere. But near the surface of the earth the atmosphere is dense and heavy. Here, in the lower atmosphere, you continually see the everchanging, dramatic, often violent weather show.

But it takes more than air to make weather. If the earth's atmosphere were never heated, mixed, or moved about, there would be no weather—or, more properly, there would be no changes in the weather. There would be no winds, no changes in air pressure, no storms, rain, or snow.

Heat is the spoon that mixes the atmosphere to make weather. All weather changes are brought about by temperature changes in different parts of the atmosphere.

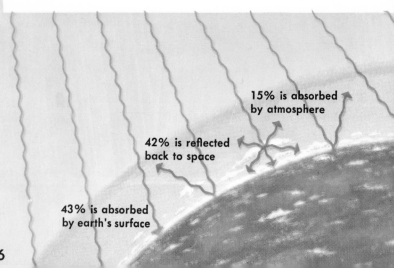

Mercury

Venus

THE SUN, source of most of the earth's heat, is a ball of glowing gases, 93 million miles away. This gigantic atomic furnace bombards the earth with 126 trillion horse-power every second. Yet this vast energy is but a half of one billionth of the sun's total output. Most of this solar energy is lost in space; traces reach other planets. The sun's energy is transmitted as waves that are similar to radio waves. Some of these are visible light waves; others are invisible. Some, although not heat waves, change to heat when absorbed by objects such as soil or our bodies. About 43 per cent of the radiation reaching our planet hits the earth's surface and is changed to heat. The rest stays in the atmosphere or is reflected into space.

15% is absorbed by atmosphere

42% is reflected back to space

43% is absorbed by earth's surface

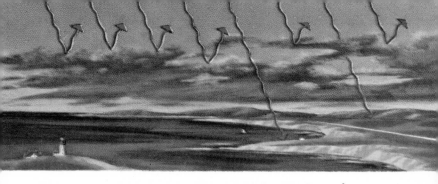

WHAT HAPPENS TO THE SUN'S HEAT is shown in the diagram above. This is for *average* weather—that is, 52 per cent cloudiness in the sky. A typical cloud reflects back into space 75 per cent of the sunlight striking it. On overcast days, only about 25 per cent of the sun's energy hits the ground. Energy that does reach the ground is absorbed and reflected in varying degrees. Snow reflects about 75 per cent, absorbs only 25 per cent; this partly accounts for the cold of polar regions. Dark forests absorb about 95 per cent of solar energy and change it to heat. Such differences in absorption and reflection account, in part, for regional differences in temperature and climate.

ABSORPTION OF SUNLIGHT BY DIFFERENT SURFACES

snow 25%

water 60—96%, depending on angle

grassy field 80 to 90%

dry sand 75%

dense forests 95%

plowed field 75 to 95%

7

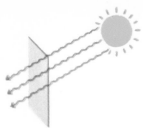

Solar rays go through glass—

heat rays cannot

A greenhouse "traps" solar radiation when "short" solar rays change to "long" heat rays.

Earth's atmosphere is like glass. It lets solar rays through but keeps most heat rays from escaping.

EARTH AS A GREENHOUSE

The glass of a greenhouse lets the short solar rays pass through. These are absorbed by objects inside and are re-radiated as long heat rays. But these long heat rays cannot get through the glass. The heat rays are continually re-absorbed and re-radiated inside. This helps keep the greenhouse warm on cold days. Some heat is lost by conduction through the glass.

Like a greenhouse, the earth's atmosphere admits most of the solar radiation. When this is absorbed by the earth's surface, it is re-radiated as heat waves, most of which are trapped by water vapor in the atmosphere. Thus the earth is kept warm.

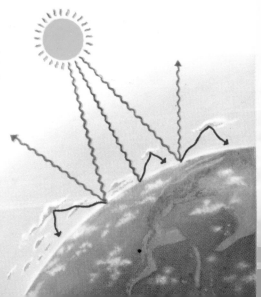

THE ATMOSPHERE AS A THER-MOSTAT controls the earth's heat as automatically as in any heating system. It protects the earth from too much solar radiation during the day, and screens out dangerous rays. It acts as an insulating blanket which keeps most of the heat from escaping at night. Without its thick atmosphere the earth would experience temperatures like the moon's. The moon's surface temperature reaches the boiling point of water (212° Fahrenheit) during the two-week lunar day. It drops to 238°F below zero during the long lunar night.

The earth cools faster on bright clear nights than on cloudy nights, because an overcast sky reflects a large amount of heat back to earth, where it is once again re-absorbed.

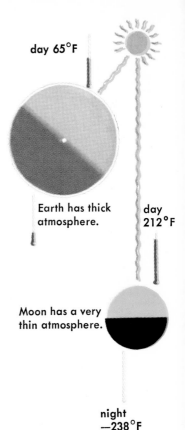

day 65°F

Earth has thick atmosphere.

day 212°F

Moon has a very thin atmosphere.

night —238°F

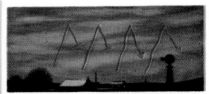

Atmosphere moderates daytime tem-

Night clouds trap the earth's heat;

perature and retards night heat loss.

on a clear night more heat escapes.

Convection currents
in heated water

HEAT AND AIR MOVEMENTS

The air is heated mainly by contact with the warm earth. When air is warmed, it expands and becomes lighter. A layer of air, warmed by contact with the earth, rises and is replaced by colder air which flows in and under it. This cold air, in turn, is warmed and rises, and it, too, is replaced by colder air. Such a circulating movement of warm and cold fluids is called "convection." You can see convection currents if you drop small bits of paper into a glass container in which water is being heated.

The air at the equator receives much more heat than the air at the poles (p. 51). So warm air at the equator rises and is replaced by colder air flowing in from north and south. The warm, light air rises and moves poleward high above the earth. As it cools, it sinks, replacing the cool surface air which has moved toward the equator. If the earth did not rotate, the air would circulate as shown. Because the earth does rotate, the circulation is different (p. 53).

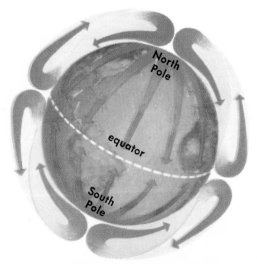

North Pole

equator

South Pole

Air movements over a
non-rotating earth

Differences in heating cause local winds.

CONVECTION causes local winds and breezes. Different land and water surfaces absorb different amounts of heat. Dark, plowed soil absorbs much more than grassy fields. Mountains absorb heat faster during daylight than nearby valleys, and lose it faster at night. Land warms faster than does water during the day and cools faster at night. The air above such surfaces is warmed or cooled accordingly —and local winds result.

Mountain breezes in daytime

Mountain breezes at night

Sea breezes in daytime

Land breezes at night

WATER IN THE ATMOSPHERE   Water is always present in the air. It evaporates from the earth, of which 70 per cent is covered with water. In the air, water exists in three states: solid, liquid, and invisible vapor.

The amount of water vapor in the air is called the "humidity." The "relative humidity" is the amount of vapor the air is holding expressed as a percentage of the amount the air could hold at that particular temperature. Warm air can hold more water than cold. When air with a given amount of water vapor cools, its relative humidity goes up; when the air is warmed, its relative humidity drops.

As the table below shows, air at 86°F is "saturated" when it holds 30.4 grams of water vapor per cubic meter. (In other words, it has a relative humidity of 100 per cent; it has reached its dew point.) But air at 68° is saturated when it holds only 17.3 grams per cubic meter. That's a difference of 13.1 grams per cubic meter. So every cubic meter of 86° saturated air that is cooled to 68° will lose 13.1 grams of water vapor as cloud droplets which, if conditions are right, will fall as rain or snow.

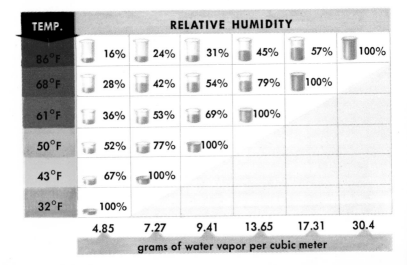

TEMP.	RELATIVE HUMIDITY					
86°F	16%	24%	31%	45%	57%	100%
68°F	28%	42%	54%	79%	100%	
61°F	36%	53%	69%	100%		
50°F	52%	77%	100%			
43°F	67%	100%				
32°F	100%					
	4.85	7.27	9.41	13.65	17.31	30.4

grams of water vapor per cubic meter

HEAT AND ATMOSPHERIC WATER

Heat evaporates millions of tons of water into the air daily. Lakes, streams, and oceans send up a steady stream of water vapor. An amazing amount of water transpires from the leaves of green plants. A single apple tree may move 1,800 gallons of water into the air in a six-month growing season.

As moist warm air rises, it slowly cools. Finally it cools so much that its relative humidity reaches 100 per cent. Clouds form and, under certain conditions, rain or snow comes down. This eternal process of evaporation, condensation, and precipitation is called the water cycle.

HOW CLOUDS ARE FORMED

When air is cooled below its saturation point the water vapor in it condenses to form clouds. When water vapor at a teakettle spout is cooled by the air around it, a small cloud forms. Your warm moist breath forms a miniature cloud when it hits the cold winter air. The clouds you see nearly every day form in several ways but all form by the same general process—cooling of air below its saturation point.

Earth radiates heat rapidly on clear nights. Air in contact with cold earth may cool below its saturation point and form low clouds, or fog (a cloud on the ground). ▶

◀ Warm air may move over a cold surface and be cooled below its saturation point. Clouds may form as warm lake or ocean air moves in over a cooler land surface.

Warm air is often lifted by a heavier mass of cold air which pushes under it like a wedge. Clouds form as warm air cools below its saturation point. ▶

Air may be heated by contact with the earth's warm surface. It expands, becomes lighter, and rises. Expansion lowers its temperature. The more it rises, the more it cools—at a rate of about 5½°F for each 1,000 ft. of rise. This "adiabatic cooling" occurs whenever air rises. Most clouds form because of adiabatic cooling.

Air moving up a slope loses heat adiabatically as it rises. If it rises enough to cool below its saturation point, clouds will form.

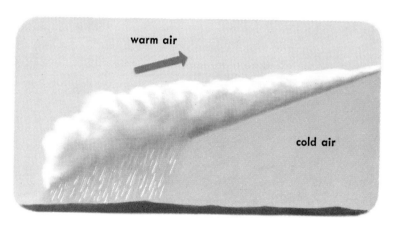

warm air

cold air

Warm air often pushes over a mass of cold air (above). Clouds may form as it cools adiabatically because of its rise.

Sometimes rain or snow from high clouds may fall through warm air, cool it, and cause lower clouds to form. These lower clouds will generally be in layers—often in several levels.

Cumulus clouds   Stratus clouds

CLOUD CLASSIFICATION • Clouds are classified according to how they are formed. There are two basic types: (1) Clouds formed by rising air currents. These are piled up and puffy. They are called "cumulus," which means piled up or accumulated. (2) Clouds formed when a layer of air is cooled below the saturation point without vertical movement. These are in sheets or foglike layers. They are called "stratus," meaning sheetlike or layered.

Clouds are further classified by altitude into four families: high clouds, middle clouds, low clouds, and towering clouds. The bases of the latter may be as low as the typical low clouds, but the tops may be at or above 75,000 ft.

CLOUD NAMES • The names of clouds are descriptive of their type and form. The word "nimbus," meaning rain cloud, is added to the names of clouds which typically produce rain or snow. The prefix "fracto-," meaning fragment, is added to names of wind-blown clouds that are broken into pieces. "Alto-," meaning high, is used to indicate middle-layer high clouds of either stratus or cumulus types. The pictures and captions on the next four pages will help you to identify major cloud types and to understand better their relationship to the weather.

16

HIGH CLOUDS are composed almost entirely of tiny ice crystals. Their bases average about 20,000 ft. above the earth. Three types exist:

Cirrus clouds, thin, wispy, and feathery, are composed entirely of ice crystals. Cirrus clouds usually form at 25,000 ft. and above, where the temperature is always far below freezing. These clouds are frequently blown about into feathery strands called "mares' tails."

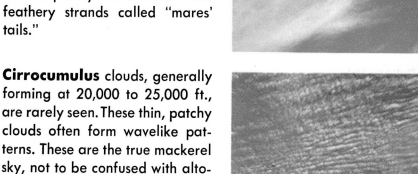

Cirrocumulus clouds, generally forming at 20,000 to 25,000 ft., are rarely seen. These thin, patchy clouds often form wavelike patterns. These are the true mackerel sky, not to be confused with altocumulus rolls. They are often rippled and always too thin to show shadows.

Cirrostratus clouds form at the same altitudes as cirrocumulus. These are thin sheets that look like fine veils or torn, wind-blown patches of gauze. Because they are made of ice crystals, cirrostratus clouds form large halos, or luminous circles, around sun and moon.

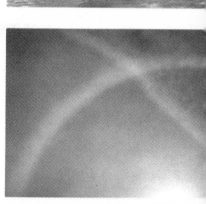

MIDDLE CLOUDS are basically stratus or cumulus. Their bases average about 10,000 ft. above the earth.

Altostratus (above) are dense veils or sheets of gray or blue. They often appear fibrous or lightly striped. The sun or moon does not form a halo, as with higher, ice-crystal cirrostratus, but appears as if seen through frosted glass.

Altocumulus (below) are patches or layers of puffy or roll-like clouds, gray or whitish. They resemble cirrocumulus, but the puffs or rolls are larger and made of water droplets, not ice crystals. Through altocumulus the sun often produces a corona, or disk, generally pale blue or yellow inside, reddish outside. The corona's color and spread distinguish it from the cirrostratus halo—a larger ring, covering much more of the sky.

LOW CLOUDS have bases that range in height from near the earth's surface to 6,500 ft. There are three main kinds:

Stratus is a low, quite uniform sheet, like fog, with the base above the ground. Dull-gray stratus clouds often make a heavy, leaden sky. Only fine drizzle can fall from true stratus clouds, because there is little or no vertical movement in them.

Nimbostratus are the true rain clouds. Darker than ordinary stratus, they have a wet look, and streaks of rain often extend to the ground. They often are accompanied by low scud clouds (fractostratus) when the wind is strong.

Stratocumulus are irregular masses of clouds spread out in a rolling or puffy layer. Gray with darker shading, stratocumulus do not produce rain but sometimes change into nimbostratus, which do. The rolls or masses then fuse together and the lower surface becomes indistinct with rain.

Cumulonimbus are the familiar thunderheads. Bases may almost touch the ground; violent updrafts may carry the tops to 75,000 ft. Winds aloft often mold the tops into a flat anvil-like form. In their most violent form these clouds produce tornadoes (p. 102).

Cumulus are puffy, cauliflower-like. Shapes constantly change. Over land, cumulus usually form by day in rising warm air, and disappear at night. They mean fair weather unless they pile up into cumulonimbus.

Cumulus and Cumulonimbus are both clouds of vertical development, unlike the layered clouds described on previous pages. Clouds of the cumulus type result from strong vertical currents. They form at almost any altitude, with bases sometimes as high as 14,000 ft.

CLOUD SYMBOLS			
⌓	cumulus	∠	altostratus
⌄	stratocumulus	⌣	altocumulus
—	stratus	⌐	cirrus
⌓	cumulonimbus	⊿	cirrostratus
⟋	nimbostratus	⌇	cirrocumulus

Rain, Snow, Dew, and Frost

PRECIPITATION such as rain, snow, sleet, and hail can occur only if there are clouds in the sky. But not all kinds of clouds can produce precipitation. Temperature, the presence of tiny foreign particles, or of ice crystals, all help determine whether precipitation will occur and what form it will take. For example, snow will not form unless air is supersaturated (cooled below its saturation point or dew point without its water vapor condensing) and is considerably below the freezing point of water.

WHAT MAKES IT RAIN? • Rain falls from clouds for the same reason anything falls to earth. The earth's gravity pulls it. But every cloud is made of water droplets or ice crystals. Why doesn't rain or snow fall constantly from all clouds? The droplets or ice crystals in clouds are exceedingly small. The effect of gravity on them is minute. Air currents move and lift droplets so that the net downward movement is zero, even though the droplets are in constant motion.

Droplets and ice crystals behave somewhat like dust in the air made visible in a shaft of sunlight. But dust particles are much larger than water droplets, and they finally fall. The cloud droplet of average size is only 1/2500 inch in diameter. It is so small that it would take 16 hours to fall half a mile in perfectly still air, and it does not fall out of moving air at all. Only when the droplet grows to a diameter of 1/125 inch or larger can it fall from the cloud. The average raindrop contains a million times as much water as a tiny cloud droplet. The growth of a cloud droplet to a size large enough to fall out is the cause of rain and other forms of precipitation. This important growth process is called "coalescence."

Cloud droplets (enlarged 70 times).   Smallest raindrop (enlarged 70 tim

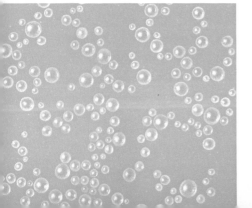

Coalescence occurs chiefly in two ways: (1) Droplets in clouds are of different sizes. Big drops move more slowly in turbulent air and in paths different from the paths of small droplets. Bigger, heavier drops are not whipped around so rapidly. So drops collide, become bigger, and finally drop as rain. This is probably the main cause of rainfall from nimbostratus and other low clouds.

1

(2) The most important type of coalescence occurs when tiny ice crystals and water droplets occur together (as near the middle of cumulonimbus clouds). Some water droplets evaporate and then condense on the crystals. The crystals grow until they drop as snow or ice pellets. As these drop through warm air, they change into raindrops.

2

(3) Lightning discharges in a thunderstorm form oxides of nitrogen that are extremely hygroscopic (water-absorbing). These oxides are added to the atmosphere and become one of the kinds of nuclei for future condensation and eventual coalescence and rainfall. But the two processes mentioned above are the main and perhaps the only causes of coalescence and hence precipitation. Research may show other possibilities.

3

SNOW Very small particles in the air may act as nuclei upon which water vapor will crystallize to form snow. Air must be supersaturated with water vapor and below the freezing point. Microscopic bits of soil, clay, sand, and ash are common nuclei. Cloud temperatures must generally be from $+10°$ to $-4°$F before snow begins to form. Vapor changes to snow even without nuclei at high altitudes in supersaturated air at $-38°$F.

SNOW PELLETS (or granular snow) are white, and of various shapes. Although much like soft hail, pellets are too small and soft to bounce. A single pellet generally forms from many supercooled cloud droplets which freeze together into crystalline form.

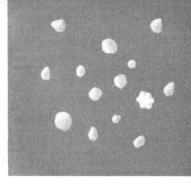

Snow pellets—magnified 3 times.

ICE PRISMS form hexagonal plates, columns, and needles that sometimes glitter like diamonds as they are blown about. Because of their small size they fall very slowly. Ice needles often make halos around sun or moon. In very cold climates ice-needle fogs form on the ground.

Ice needles—magnified 10 times.

Halo caused by ice needles.

ICE PELLETS (sleet) consist of transparent or translucent beads of ice. Sleet occurs when rain, dropping from upper warm air, falls through a layer of freezing air. Raindrops first become freezing rain (supercooled) and when striking the ground in this condition form glaze (p. 27). But further cooling produces ice pellets, or true sleet, which bounces on hitting the ground.

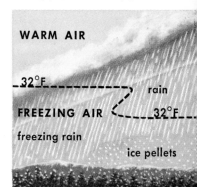

WARM AIR

32°F

rain

FREEZING AIR

32°F

freezing rain

ice pellets

Ice pellets—magnified 3 times.

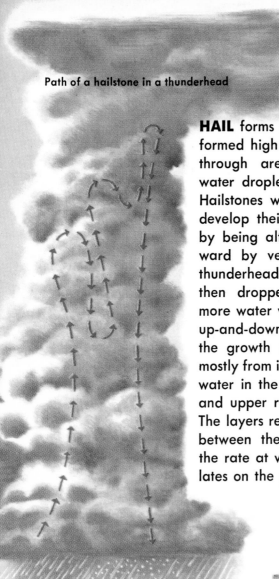

Path of a hailstone in a thunderhead

HAIL forms as frozen raindrops, formed high in the clouds, move through areas of supercooled water droplets in thunderclouds. Hailstones were long thought to develop their onionlike structure by being alternately forced upward by vertical winds in the thunderhead to a freezing level, then dropped down to where more water was picked up. Such up-and-down trips do occur, but the growth of hailstones results mostly from ice pellets' picking up water in the supercooled middle and upper regions of the cloud. The layers result from differences between the freezing rate and the rate at which water accumulates on the pellets.

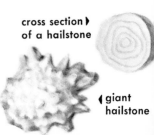

cross section ▶
of a hailstone

◀ giant
hailstone

ICE STORMS are characterized by glaze. Glaze is as destructive as it is beautiful. It occurs when rain or drizzle that has been supercooled (cooled below 32°F but not yet frozen) falls on cold surfaces and immediately freezes. Glaze ice formed from this freezing rain can snap branches, wires, and poles and cause hazardous driving conditions.

DEW does not fall. It is water vapor that condenses on solid surfaces that have cooled below the condensation point of the air in contact with them. This cooling by radiation occurs usually on clear nights. The "sweat" that forms on the outside of a glass of cold lemonade on a hot day is also dew.

FROST is formed like dew but at temperatures below freezing. The water vapor changes directly to small, fine frost crystals without condensing into water drops first. Frost crystals growing on windows develop feathery patterns as the primary frost melts and recrystallizes.

Drainage pattern of the United States and Canada.

WHAT HAPPENS TO RAIN AND SNOW   Rain either is stored in the ground, ponds, or lakes, or runs off to be stored in the ocean. It eventually evaporates into the air again. Surface runoff of precipitation and the underground flow of water give us our brooks, streams, and rivers. Rivers always flow from higher to lower levels, cutting their own valleys. Streams and rivers merge and finally they empty into the oceans. When the supply of water is larger than the amount normally handled by streams and rivers, flooding occurs. In areas of hard, baked ground or clay soil, the runoff from a thunderstorm is almost complete, since there is little seepage into the soil. Flash floods may result. Water may also run underground, to emerge as springs. Wells tap this underground water, which provides many areas with an abundant supply. Large underground rivers exist, but these are rare.

29

Water is stored as snow and ice, as well as in lakes.

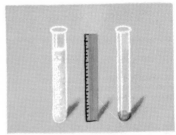

Ten inches of snow melts into one inch of water.

WATER STORAGE Lakes and ponds obviously store a great deal of water. Not so obvious is the immense reservoir of water stored in the polar ice caps, in glaciers, and in snow on mountains and on the cold northern plains during winter. Winter snows in the mountains determine the water supply for irrigation and for power use. This snow melts with the spring thaw and fills the rivers. If spring is late, the melting will be more sudden, resulting in floods.

GROUND WATER Topsoil holds an immense amount of water. Some of this is transferred into the air by green plants. But most of it seeps through soil and porous rock until it reaches nonporous clay or rock. It forms a massive subterranean reservoir, filling all the cracks and pores in the rock and soil. The underground water, like surface water, flows downhill and seeps out into streams or comes out in springs. Eventually this water, too, evaporates or reaches the sea.

well

water table →

spring

river

porous soil and rock

impervious rock

RAINMAKING is an ancient hope, a 19th-century fake, and a modern scientific fact. Every primitive tribe has tried one way or another to make it rain. Primitive magic, rain dances, and sacrifices have all been used to induce rain. By coincidence, rain has followed these efforts often enough to keep alive the belief in the efficiency of the methods. Quite a boom in rainmaking developed in the 19th century. Drums were beaten, cannons shot, and explosives were set off, producing great quantities of smoke. The methods were worthless and so were many of the operators. One of the smoothest of these confidence men used U. S. Weather Bureau climatological data. He never appeared in a drought area until it was almost certain that rain was but a few days away. Then he would put on his act, wait for the rain, and collect his fee.

Modern rainmaking techniques are based on known facts of coalescence and genuinely influence rainfall and snowfall (see pp. 32-33). All modern techniques depend upon the "seeding" of artificial nuclei into potential rain clouds. Silver iodide crystals are most commonly used.

Hopi Indians dance for rain.

19th-century rainmakers.

Silver iodide generator.

Dry ice dropped from plane forms partly cleared strip in stratus clouds.

MODERN RAINMAKING grew out of studies of how aircraft collect ice on wings and other surfaces. Dr. Vincent J. Schaefer was attempting to prevent the formation of supercooled clouds (which cause ice to form on aircraft). He discovered that tiny bits of dry ice (frozen carbon dioxide) produced fantastic numbers of ice nuclei when "seeded" into clouds colder than 32°F. A piece of dry ice the size of a grain of rice caused the formation of more than a trillion ice crystals. Each grew at the expense of supercooled cloud droplets and formed snow (see p. 23). The technique of seeding supercooled clouds has since been used to lessen ground fogs and, under certain conditions, to induce snow or rainfall from large cumulus clouds. Dr. Irving Langmuir and Dr. Bernard Vonnegut pioneered further studies by seeding clouds with water and silver iodide. The water initiates coalescence. Since the silver iodide has a molecular structure nearly identical with that of ice, it induces coalescence in much the same manner as ice crystals would.

CLOUD SEEDING experiments continued with miniature clouds produced under laboratory conditions. Various substances were sprayed into a cold chamber in an effort to produce ice crystals or coalescence. Dry ice and silver iodide both worked well. Finely ground dry ice (with a temperature of −108°F) caused cloud droplets to crystallize along its path. These crystals grew rapidly at the ex-

Seeding a cumulus cloud with dry ice.

pense of the water droplets around them, and soon became large enough to fall. Silver iodide, on the other hand, acted directly as a nucleus for ice formation. These ice crystals, also, grew until they fell.

Clouds are now seeded with either dry ice or silver iodide. One pound of dry ice spread by a plane may start a shower in large cumulus clouds. Silver iodide is less expensive to use, because it can be sent up from the ground to clouds from special generators. But cloud seeding is not successful unless conditions are nearly right for natural precipitation. Seeding can induce rain under the right conditions. It can cause more rain to fall than would occur with undisturbed natural conditions. It cannot produce rain from fair-weather cumulus clouds. Nor is it yet possible for cloud seeding, which is still in its infancy, to induce rain to fall over a widespread area.

Man-made snow cloud in a cold chamber.

NASA

The Atmosphere

The earth's atmosphere has been photographed from space by artificial satellites and astronauts since 1961. The first pictures taken from 400 miles up by weather satellites confirmed the guesses of meteorologists about how cloud patterns would appear. The picture above was taken by a satellite 22,300 miles above the earth. The oceans directly below the satellite appear dark blue. Near the edges of the picture, scattering by atmospheric gases causes the bright blue appearance. The bright white clouds are arranged in swirls, bands, and clusters that show the positions of lows (p. 60), fronts (p. 77), and convection (pp. 10, 14).

A full understanding of the weather requires knowledge of the atmosphere. We live at the bottom of a virtual ocean of air. Extending upward perhaps 1,000 miles, this massive, restless ocean is far different, and far more tempestuous, than the watery oceans that cover three-fourths of the globe. A narrow band of compacted air lying just above the earth is the region of continuous winds. Here, the rising and falling air currents sometimes develop into violent storms. Only recently have the most advanced aircraft ventured above this thin layer, some 5 to 11 miles thick.

The ocean of air differs in one major way from an ocean of water. Water is nearly incompressible. A cubic foot of water on an ocean bottom weighs much the same as a cubic foot near the surface. But the air of the atmospheric ocean is highly compressible: a cubic foot of air at the surface weighs billions of times as much as a cubic foot at the outer edge of the atmosphere. The atmosphere thins so rapidly as one leaves the earth that, only 3½ miles up, over half the atmosphere by weight would lie below you. It is chiefly in this 3½-mile blanket of heavy air that weather changes are born. The atmosphere 500 miles out is so thin that there are only about 22 million molecules of air per cubic inch, compared to billions upon billions at the earth's surface. Still farther out, the ever-thinning atmosphere blends with the stray gases and dust of outer space.

about 1,000 miles

Half the weight of the atmosphere is packed into the bottom 3½ miles.

Composition of air
at altitudes above·
500 miles

hydrogen 50%

helium 50%

Composition of air
at altitudes up to
about 45 miles

nitrogen 78%

oxygen 21%

argon 0.93%
carbon dioxide 0.03%
all other gases 0.04%

AIR CONSISTS MAINLY OF GASES

that will not directly sustain life. Oxygen, which all living things need, makes up slightly less than 21 per cent of the air. Inert nitrogen makes up 78 per cent. The remainder of the gases, all totaling less than 1 per cent, are carbon dioxide, argon, neon, radon, helium, krypton, xenon, hydrogen, methane, nitrous oxide, and ozone (a form of oxygen). Besides these, air contains up to 4 per cent water vapor, also dust and gases such as smoke, salt, other chemicals from sea spray or industry, carbon monoxide, and micro-organisms.

If the air were perfectly quiet, the heavier particles and gases would settle close to the earth and the lightest would be found the farthest out from earth's surface. But the constant motion of the air near the surface mixes the gases so that the same proportions exist from the earth's surface up to about 45 miles. Farther out are found chiefly the lighter gases. Probably only the lightest gases, helium and hydrogen, are found at heights above 500 miles. In intermediate levels are found high concentrations of ozone and ionized nitrogen, together with smaller quantities of other ionized gases. Ozone, by absorption, plays a large part in the earth's heat balance— as does the increasing amount of man-made carbon dioxide.

THE ATMOSPHERE consists of five layers. First and most important is the troposphere, which lies closest to earth. Next above is the stratosphere. Where the troposphere ends and the stratosphere begins is a boundary called the tropopause, which averages 5 miles above the earth near the poles, and 11 miles above at the equator. The stratosphere goes up to about 30 miles. Above this is the mesosphere, extending to about 50 miles. The thermosphere above contains layers of ionized particles that reflect long radio waves back to earth. At about 500 miles the exosphere starts; little is known about this layer.

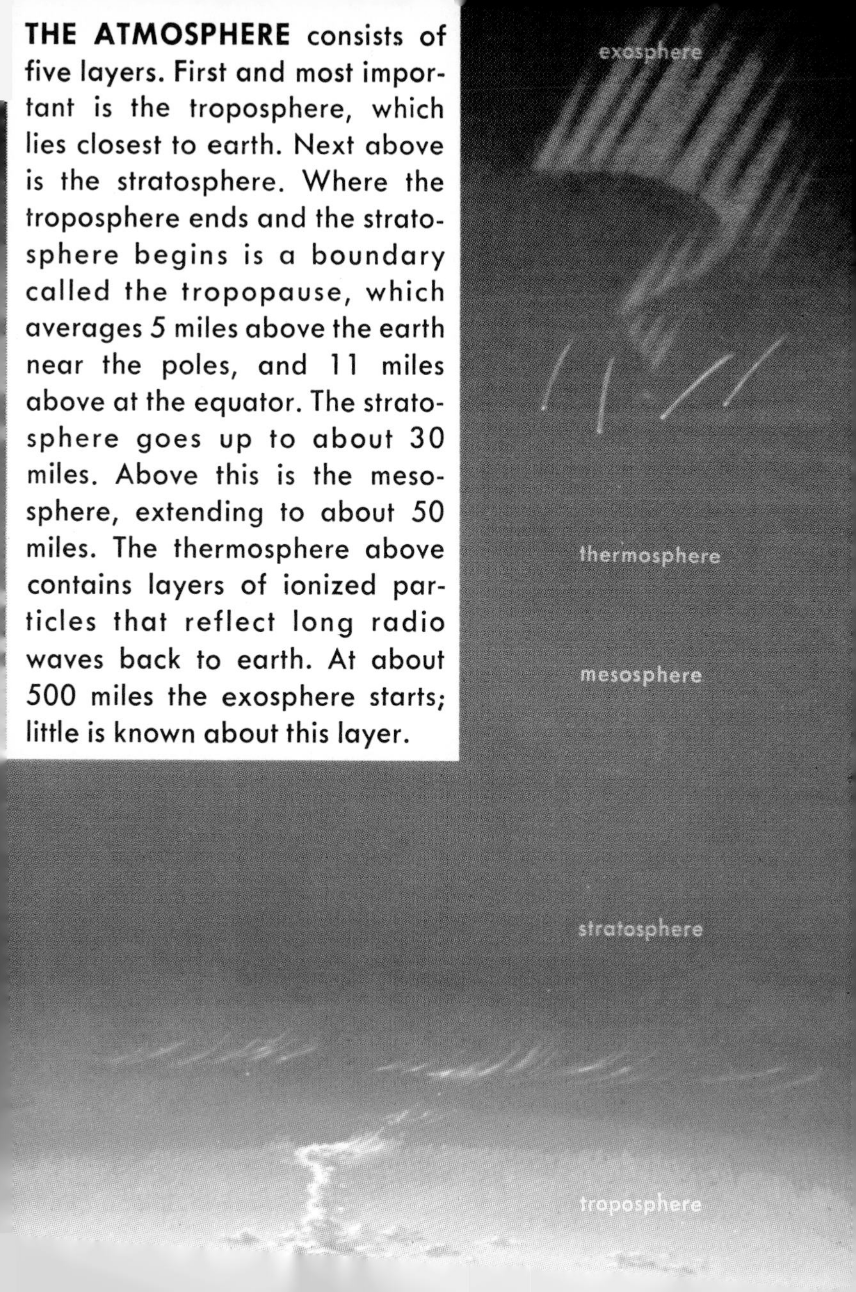

exosphere

thermosphere

mesosphere

stratosphere

troposphere

THE TROPOSPHERE—WEATHER BREEDER In this layer are nearly all of the clouds. Here is where weather occurs. Air, heated by contact with the earth, rises and is replaced by colder air. These vertical currents create horizontal winds at or near the surface of the earth. Water, evaporated from the land and seas, rises with the ascending warm air. As the air rises, the surrounding pressure lessens, so it steadily expands. Expansion is a cooling process (see below). If the air rises high enough, it cools until condensation forms clouds.

Expansion of any gas is a cooling process. Compression creates heat. The cylinder and hose of a tire pump get hot as air is pumped and compressed. The sudden expansion of gas rushing out of an aerosol bomb cools the tip.

Most air conditioners work on the same principle, as shown below. A gas is compressed in the part outside the house. The heat of compression is given off to the outside air, and the gas condenses to a liquid. The liquid is forced through a tiny nozzle and expands suddenly in the coils inside the house. This expansion (and evaporation back to a gas) cools the coils and also the air which is blown over the coils into the room.

HOW AN AIR CONDITIONER WORKS

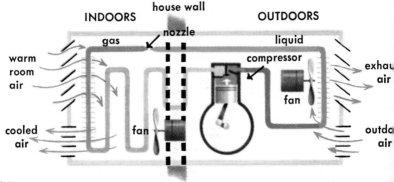

38

7000 ft.	41.5°F
6000 ft.	47°F
5000 ft.	52.5°F
4000 ft.	58°F
3000 ft.	63.5°F
2000 ft.	69°F
1000 ft.	74.5°F

Adiabatic temperature changes as air travels over a mountain.

The troposphere has a kind of automatic air conditioner. The primary heat pump is, of course, the sun. It heats the earth's surface which, in turn, heats the air in contact with it. The air expands, becomes lighter, and rises. But the higher it rises the more it expands, because the pressure around it is steadily lessening. And the more it expands, the more it cools. This is an automatic cooling process which occurs without any loss of heat due to outside causes. The rising air cools automatically at about 5½°F for each 1,000 ft. it rises. This is what happens when air rises up the side of a mountain. When it goes down the other side, it begins compressing. It warms up in doing so at the same rate (5½°F per 1,000 ft.) it cooled in rising. This automatic temperature change in rising or falling air is called "adiabatic" warming or cooling. Air need not be pushed up by a mountain for this adiabatic change to take place. Air rising over heated plains will also cool at the same rate of about 5½°F per 1,000 ft. rise.

39

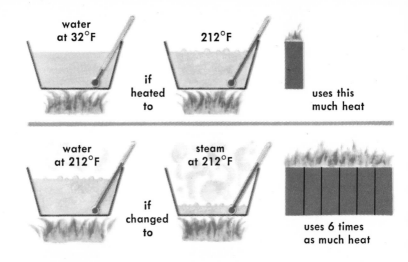

water at 32°F — if heated to — 212°F — uses this much heat

water at 212°F — if changed to — steam at 212°F — uses 6 times as much heat

CONDENSATION complicates adiabatic cooling and warming, and makes the temperatures on the windward side of mountain ranges lower than those on the leeward side. Mainly because of condensation, there are relatively cool valleys west of the Sierra Nevadas and hot deserts to the east.

Considerable heat is needed to change liquid water to water vapor. Heat increases the speed of water molecules, so that many more escape as water vapor. Changing a pan of water at the boiling point to vapor requires six times the heat needed to raise the same amount of water from freezing to boiling. When water vapor condenses back into liquid water, the same large amount of heat is given off. This heat can increase the temperature of the air considerably. When air is rising, two opposing influences operate as its moisture condenses: adiabatic cooling tends to lower its temperature; and heat of condensation tends to raise it. The net effect is an average cooling of 3.2°F per 1,000 ft. of rise when condensation occurs.

Take an example: Air at 60°F moves up the west side of a mountain. It cools adiabatically 5.5°F for each

1,000 ft. of rise up to the clouds at 4,000 ft. As condensation begins, heat is released, and the adiabatic cooling is thus partly offset. From 4,000 ft. to the mountain top, at 10,000 ft., the net cooling is only 3.2°F per 1,000 ft. Thus the total cooling of the wind as it sweeps up the mountain is

4 x 5.5, or 22°	from valley floor to cloud base
plus 6 x 3.2, or 19.2°	from cloud base to mountain top
Total 41.2°	from valley to mountain top

The air that began at 60°F tops the mountain at 18.8°F.

As the air pours down the eastern slope, it compresses and warms, adiabatically, at the rate of 5.5°F per 1,000 ft. Because of the warming, no further condensation occurs. Total warming of the air from mountain top to valley, 10,000 ft. below, is 10 x 5.5°F, or 55°F. Adding this to the mountain top temperature of 18.8°F gives 73.8°F as the temperature of the eastern valley. The temperature at the eastern foot of the mountain is 13.8°F higher than at the western foot. Condensation and precipitation on the western slope made the difference.

Chinook winds are an example of this down-slope warming of air. They occur on the eastern slope of the Rockies, often with dramatic effect. One Chinook brought the temperature up from −6°F to 37°F in 15 minutes.

Condensation modifies adiabatic cooling.

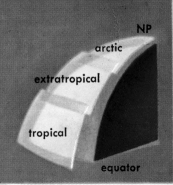

Overlapping leaves of the tropopause.

Typical jet stream paths.

TROPOPAUSE AND JET STREAM The tropopause—the zone that marks the end of the troposphere and the beginning of the nearly weatherless stratosphere—was once thought to be continuous from poles to equator. We now know that the tropopause has breaks, giving it an overlapping, leaf-like structure. These breaks are important in connection with the jet streams. A jet stream is a tubular ribbon of high-speed winds, generally from the west and some 20,000 to 40,000 feet up. Jet streams form at the overlaps, particularly of the arctic tropopause and the extratropical tropopause. They are at least partially the result of the strong temperature contrast there.

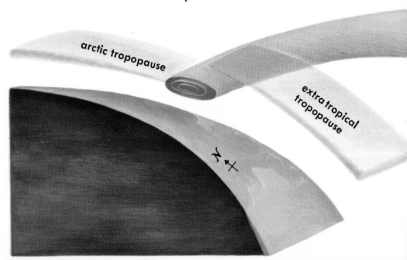

A jet stream was discovered by American B-29 pilots flying to Japan from the Marianas in World War II. They consistently reported westerly winds with speeds far in excess of those expected. A jet stream is usually about 300 miles wide and 4 miles high. At its core it averages 100 miles per hour in winter and 50 miles per hour in summer; these speeds may rise to 250 miles per hour or more. Forming a wavy path at the top of the troposphere, the jet stream assists high-flying airplanes traveling east; planes going west try to avoid these strong headwinds. The strength of the jet winds decreases outward from the core, and from place to place in the stream. The number of jet streams and their paths varies from day to day and season to season. A typical jet stream has areas of maximum winds along it that tend to travel eastward. Two places where these wind maximums occur with great frequency are across Japan and over the New England states. In winter, over the North American Continent, there are three major jet streams: one over northern Canada, one over the United States, and one over the subtropics.

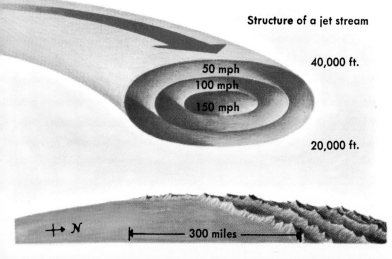

Structure of a jet stream

50 mph
100 mph
150 mph

40,000 ft.

20,000 ft.

N

300 miles

THE STRATOSPHERE is the almost weatherless part of the atmosphere. It extends from the tropopause upward about 30 miles. The name suggests its nature, for it usually has very little vertical air movement; it is a uniform layer, or stratum. Temperature drops much more slowly with height than in the troposphere. In fact, the temperature begins to rise again near the top of this layer. Flying in the stratosphere is generally smooth, and the visibility is always excellent. The air is thin and offers very little resistance to a plane; hence a gallon of fuel carries a plane much farther through the stratosphere. A region of no weather, the stratosphere is preferred by jet pilots, for here they can fly at top speeds with little fear of turbulence. Often too far above us to be seen, the jets chalk their path across the sky as moisture from their engines forms condensation trails—streaks of fine ice crystals in an otherwise weatherless atmosphere.

THE MESOSPHERE lies above the stratosphere, extending upward to 50 miles. Temperature decreases from a high of about 30°F at the top of the stratosphere to a low near —100°F at the top of the mesosphere.

THE THERMOSPHERE, once called the ionosphere, is the next layer up; the air is extremely thin. The scattered air particles are ionized, or electrified by removal of electrons (negatively charged particles). This ionization is caused by constant bombardment of air particles by cosmic rays from outer space. This ionized air forms in layers that reflect radio waves back to earth, making it possible for us to receive radio waves from beyond the horizon. These radio-wave-reflecting layers are the Kennelly-Heaviside or E Layer, 50 to 80 miles up; the F Layer, 150 to 200 miles up; and a variable number of other layers that result from splitting of the E and F layers.

The extreme temperatures in the thermosphere are probably caused by absorption of solar energy by atomic oxygen. Estimates put the temperatures (at 300 miles) in excess of 2500°F in daylight and 300°F at night. Astronauts were not broiled by these temperatures for two reasons. First the manned spacecraft were heat shielded, air conditioned, and rotated to avoid continuous exposure to the sun. Secondly, the air particles are so far apart that not enough hit the spacecraft at any time to cause an increase in the skin temperature.

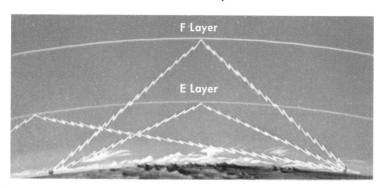

Radio waves reflected by the layers of ionized air can be received beyond the horizon.

THE EXOSPHERE is the final and highest layer of the atmosphere. Hotter even than the thermosphere's air particles, the ions of gas in the exosphere are possibly as hot as 4,500°F. They are bombarded so fiercely by cosmic rays that they exist only in atomic rather than molecular form. At night, shielded from the sun's direct rays, the temperature of the particles drops nearly to absolute zero—about −460°F.

Curtain aurora

HIGH ALTITUDE PHENOMENA

Auroras result from the action of streams of solar particles on the ionosphere, 50 to 600 miles up. What happens is much like events in a neon tube. Because the earth is a magnet, ionization is strongest near the poles, and the auroras are seen mainly at high latitudes.

Mother - of - pearl Clouds may consist of water droplets. These rare clouds appear as bands of pastel colors, 14 to 19 miles high. The sky is otherwise clear at the altitudes where they are seen. These also are known as nacreous clouds.

Noctilucent Clouds, the highest clouds known, are probably formed from meteor dust. Appearing in the western sky shortly after sunset at a height of some 50 miles, they have a gold edge near the horizon and are bluish white above. Both noctilucent and mother-of-pearl clouds travel at terrific speeds—394 miles per hour was once observed.

Meteors are visitors from outer space. They hit our atmosphere at tremendous speeds—perhaps 90,000 miles per hour. Friction with the air of the upper atmosphere heats them to incandescence, and most of them vaporize into gases or disintegrate into harmless dust before they come to within 30 miles of the earth's surface. Thus our atmosphere protects us. Millions of meteors, most of them smaller than grains of sand, hit our atmosphere every day. Very few ever reach the ground.

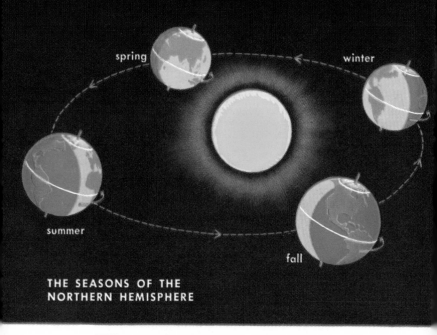

**THE SEASONS OF THE
NORTHERN HEMISPHERE**

The Earth's Motions
and Weather

The earth has five motions in space. It rotates on its axis once each 24 hours, with a slow wobble (like that of a top) which takes 26,000 years to complete. It revolves around the sun at 18½ miles per second, making the circuit in 365¼ days. It speeds with the rest of our solar system at 12 miles per second toward the star Vega. Finally, our entire galaxy, with its billions of stars, is rotating in space—our part of it at a speed of 170 miles per second.

Only two of these motions affect the weather. But their effect is profound. Earth's annual trip around the sun gives us our seasons and their typical weather. Earth's daily rotation not only results in night and day; it produces the major wind belts of our earth, and each has its typical pattern of weather.

CAUSE OF THE SEASONS Seasons result from the fact that the axis on which the earth spins is slanted 23½° to the plane of its orbit. When the North Pole is tipped toward the sun, the northern hemisphere has summer. The sun's rays beat more directly down on the northern hemisphere and the days are longer.

The sun is farthest north at the summer solstice, about June 22. Then the sun is directly over the Tropic of Cancer, and daylight hours are longest in the northern hemisphere and nights are the shortest of any time in the year. The North Pole is in the middle of its annual period of six months of sunlight, and the South Pole in the middle of its six months of relative darkness.

Summer solstice

Spring and fall equinoxes

Winter solstice

At the winter solstice (about Dec. 22) the North Pole is tipped farthest away from the sun, which is now directly over the Tropic of Capricorn. The southern hemisphere has summer; the northern hemisphere has winter. Conditions are just the reverse of those at the summer solstice. The Antarctic is now the "land of the midnight sun" and the Arctic is sunless.

At the fall and spring equinoxes (about Sept. 23 and March 21, respectively) the earth's tilt is sidewise with respect to the sun. Light falls equally on northern and southern hemispheres. Day and night are of equal duration everywhere on the earth. The equinoxes mark the beginnings of spring and fall.

SUMMER IS WARMER than winter for two reasons: the days are longer (more time for the sun to heat the earth) and the sun's rays, striking our part of the earth more directly, are therefore more concentrated.

Days and nights at the equator are always 12 hours long. The farther north you go in summer, the longer the days and the shorter the nights. This is so because the sun in summer shines across the pole. The nearer one gets to the pole, the longer the day becomes, until it finally becomes 24 hours long. To an observer in the "land of the midnight sun" the sun appears to move along the horizon instead of rising and setting.

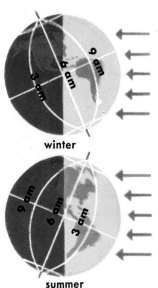

winter

summer

But as winter comes, the sun seems to move south. The farther north you go, the shorter the winter days and the longer the nights.

The sun's apparent movement relative to the earth in winter and in summer is shown below. On Dec. 22, at the latitude of Washington, D.C., the sun at noon is only about 27° above the southern horizon. The day is short because the sun's path from eastern to western horizon is short. But on June 22, at the same latitude, the sun rises farther in the north and at noon reaches about 74° altitude. Its path is longer and so daylight lasts about 15 hours.

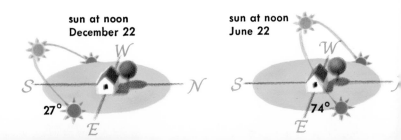

sun at noon
December 22

sun at noon
June 22

27°

74°

slanting rays spread out thinly

vertical rays cover a smaller area

To see the effect of the directness of the sun's rays, set a flashlight 1 ft. above a large sheet of paper. Mark the outline of the circle of light it makes. Now hold the flashlight at an angle to the paper—but still a foot away. Mark the outline of the ellipse of light it makes. The same amount of light hit the paper both times. But the first time it was concentrated, the second time more spread out. When the rays were direct the concentration for a unit area was greatest.

The summer sun follows a path more nearly overhead, so its rays are more concentrated. The winter sunlight hits the earth at a greater slant. The same amount of sunlight now spreads out over a larger area. In addition, winter sunlight must pass through more atmosphere, because it has a more slanted path. More energy is diffused by the atmosphere and less reaches the earth to warm it.

summer sun

winter sun

51

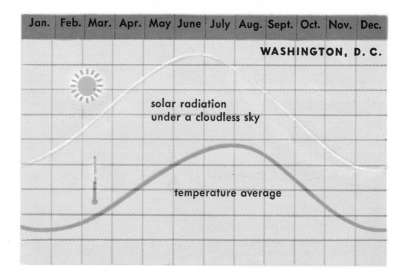

| Jan. | Feb. | Mar. | Apr. | May | June | July | Aug. | Sept. | Oct. | Nov. | Dec. |

WASHINGTON, D.C.

solar radiation
under a cloudless sky

temperature average

SEASONAL LAG August is hotter than June even though the sun is more nearly overhead and the day is longest on June 22. In terms of solar radiation reaching the earth, May, June, and July should be our warmest months. But June, July, and August actually are. Why?

During the year the earth, as a whole, loses precisely the same amount of heat it receives from the sun. But as the sun moves north in spring, our part of the earth gains heat faster than heat is lost. On June 22 it is receiving maximum solar radiation. The heat gain continues to exceed heat loss until maximum warmth is reached, usually in late July. Heat gain continues to exceed heat loss, at a diminishing rate, until about August 31. Then our part of the earth starts to lose heat faster than it receives it, and begins to cool down. The process is like starting a fire in a stove: the roaring fire heats the room slowly, but the room will stay warm for a while after the fire has died down. The same heat lag accounts for the fact that the warmest time of day is usually about 3 p.m.—not noon, when the sun's rays are most intense.

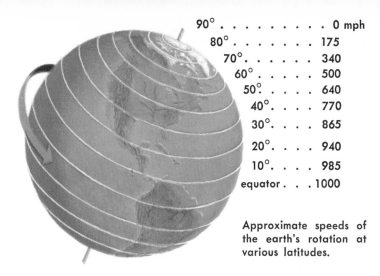

90°	0 mph
80°	175
70°	340
60°	500
50°	640
40° . . .	770
30° . . .	865
20° . . .	940
10° . . .	985
equator . . .	1000

Approximate speeds of the earth's rotation at various latitudes.

EARTH'S ROTATION AND WINDS If the earth were not rotating, heated air would rise over the equator and move north and south high above the earth's surface. It would cool and sink down at the poles. The sinking air would force air at the earth's surface toward the equator. So surface winds on a smooth non-rotating earth would all move directly toward the equator with equal speed (see p. 10).

The earth's rotation changes this. The earth at the equator is about 25,000 miles around. The earth makes one complete rotation every 24 hours. Hence every point on the equator moves eastward at a little more than 1,000 mph. But every place north or south of the equator moves more slowly to the east, simply because the distance around the earth becomes less as you go north or south of the equator. At latitude 45°, exactly halfway between the equator and the poles, the earth spins eastward at about 700 mph. At the poles there is no movement at all, since these are the ends of the earth's axis.

These differences in the earth's speed of rotation at various latitudes have a marked effect on our winds, as we shall now see.

WIND DEFLECTION is caused by the earth's rotation. This deflection, called the Coriolis Effect, is demonstrated for the northern hemisphere by the experiment below.

Place an old phonograph record on the turntable. The hole at the center represents the Noth Pole; the rim, the equator. Now spin the turntable slowly by hand counter-clockwise, the way the earth turns as viewed from above the North Pole. As the record turns, draw a line with chalk from the center hole straight away from you to the "equator" edge. See how the "easterly" rotating record causes the chalk line to curve to its right ("west" as seen from above). In the diagram, the dotted line shows the actual path of your chalk; the solid line, the mark it made on the record. Repeat the experiment, but draw a straight line from the rim of the record to the center. Again the chalk mark shows a curve to the right.

Winds on earth shift to the right exactly like the chalk line, and for the same reason. Imagine a wind from the north, starting at Chicago (latitude 45°). The top drawing on the next page shows this wind blowing straight south as viewed from above the North Pole. It moves in a straight line toward star P, and point A on the equator. But as the wind moves south, the earth (and point A along with it) is moving eastward. So the straight path, as seen from space, becomes a curved path to the right as seen by an observer on the earth's surface.

Wind deflection illustrated by phonograph record:

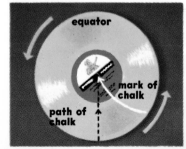

Drawings 1, 2, 3 show the wind shift as you would see it from space over the equator. The drawings show meridians (imaginary lines marking the earth into sections, like an orange). The north wind starts south along Meridian A. It moves in a straight line directly toward the equator. As the wind moves from latitude 45° to 30°, earth's eastward rotation moves Meridian A to your right, and Meridian B moves to a position directly under you. By the time the wind has reached the equator, Meridian B has moved east and has been replaced by Meridian C. As seen from space, the wind still moves directly south. But to a man on the earth, the wind has taken a curved path and is now a northeast wind.

Winds moving northward, also, curve to their right. This shift helps explain the general circulation of air over the earth.

In the southern hemisphere this effect is exactly reversed and winds shift to the left. To see why, repeat the experiment on p. 54. This time, however, turn the record clockwise, as if you were looking down on the earth from above the South Pole.

Path over rotating earth.

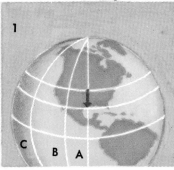

North wind at Chicago . . .

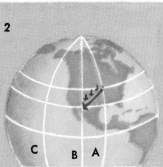

shifts to its right becoming NE.

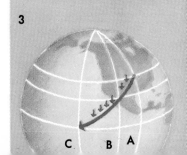

GENERAL AIR MOVEMENTS IN THE NORTHERN HEMISPHERE begin with air moving north high above the equator, and slowly shifting toward the east because of the earth's rotation. By the time this upper air has gone about one-third of the way from the equator to the North Pole, it is moving eastward. As more air from the equator arcs north and east into this region, about latitude 30°, it piles up, forming an area of high pressure. Some air is forced down to the surface of the earth. There a portion flows southward, turning west as it goes. This portion forms the so-called "trade winds" that blow rather steadily from the northeast. But some of the descending air moves northward and is deflected to the east. This air forms the prevailing westerlies which blow over the middle latitudes (30° to 60°N).

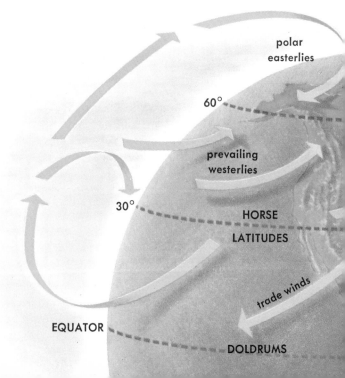

polar
easterlies

60°

prevailing
westerlies

30°

HORSE
LATITUDES

trade winds

EQUATOR

DOLDRUMS

Not all of the high air sinks to the surface at latitude 30°. Some of it continues north, high above the earth. It cools by radiation as it goes, and finally contracts and becomes so heavy that it sinks down near the North Pole. The pressure builds up in that region, and the cold, heavy air moves southward on the surface, shifting toward the west as it goes. At about latitude 60°, it runs into the prevailing westerlies traveling northeast. The line of collision is called the "polar front." The warm air from the south pushes up in a wedge over the cold, south-moving, polar air. The rising warm air is rapidly cooled, and unsettled weather conditions result. This polar front is the source of much of the changing weather in the United States. The air mass breaks through in cold waves that may move as far south as Florida and Mexico.

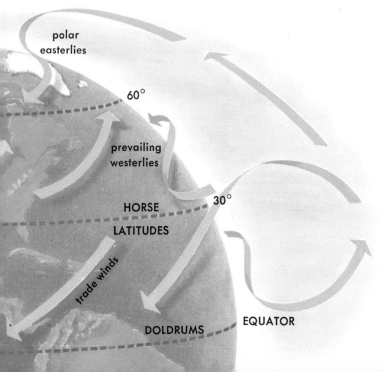

polar easterlies

60°

prevailing westerlies

HORSE LATITUDES

30°

trade winds

DOLDRUMS

EQUATOR

THE EARTH'S GENERAL CIRCULATION, its wind and weather, are modified by many things, such as winds caused by uneven local heating, differences in heat absorption of oceans and land, and seasonal changes. But some general conditions are worth noting—as, for example, that the circulation in the southern hemisphere is the opposite of circulation in the northern. Winds shift to the left for the same reason that winds north of the equator shift to the right. Northern hemisphere wind patterns exist in the southern hemisphere, but reversed. Each pattern has its near counterpart in the southern hemisphere.

GENERAL WIND CIRCULATION

N.P.

60°N

polar easterlies

prevailing westerlies

30°N

northeast trades

equator

southeast trades

prevailing westerlies

30°S

polar easterlies

60°S

S.P.

Note reversal of winds in southern hemisphere

The Equatorial Doldrums As surface air moves toward the equator with the north and south trade winds, it is heated by the direct rays of the sun, and rises. Rising air creates the equatorial calms, or doldrums. Day after day, week after week may go by without a breeze. Sailing ships avoided this region when possible. From the rising moist air of this region tropical typhoons, or hurricanes, are born in summer (p. 107). Here also occurs heavy tropical rainfall.

The Trade Winds are well named, for these steady northeast winds marked a popular route for sailing vessels. Even now, aircraft traveling west in this zone have a tail wind much of the time. Skies are clear near latitude 30° but cloudiness and heavy, frequent, showery rainfall occur nearer the equator, where the air rises at the doldrum zone.

The Horse Latitudes are another region of calm. As the air sinks, and thus warms adiabatically, skies tend to be cloudless. Winds are weak and undependable. The term "horse latitudes" apparently originated because sailing ships carrying horses from Spain to the New World often became becalmed and ran out of food and water for the animals. The sea was sometimes littered with bodies of starved horses which had been thrown overboard.

The Prevailing Westerlies The major air flow over the United States is from slightly south of west to slightly north of west. Were it not for the repeated invasions of cold air from the polar front, and complications caused by air being forced over mountains, weather in the United States would be rather stable because of these winds—fair weather and clear skies alternating with steady rains as the air moved north and slowly cooled. But the polar front and other factors cause rapid and often violent weather changes.

The Polar Easterlies Bounded on the south by the polar front, the zone of the polar easterlies is one of cold air moving southwest until it runs into the prevailing westerlies. The front itself moves as these two air masses push back and forth. At the front, warm, moist air from the south is lifted over the heavier, cold air. Bad weather results.

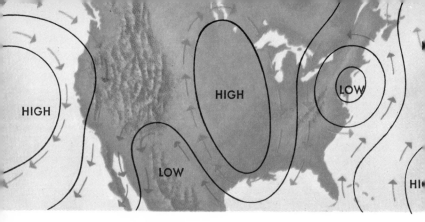

Highs and Lows

HIGHS AND LOWS Unequal heating of the earth between the equator and the poles causes north-south winds. Rotation of the earth turns these east or westward, depending on the hemisphere. This shifting of great masses of moving air creates the overall pattern of air circulation. But it does something else. It creates whirling masses of air called high-pressure cells, or *highs,* and low-pressure cells, or *lows.* The highs (anticyclones) generally bring fair weather. The lows (cyclones) bring unsettled weather. In the region of the prevailing westerlies (latitude 30° to 60°) high cells follow a general path from west to east (moved by the prevailing westerlies) and alternate with low cells which they generate and drive along. The table below summarizes the important facts:

	HIGHS	**LOWS**
Weather:	Generally fair	Generally cloudy, with rain or snow
Circulation:	Clockwise in northern hemisphere Counterclockwise in southern hemisphere	Counterclockwise in northern hemisphere Clockwise in southern hemisphere
Winds:	Light	Strong
Temperature:	Warm or cold for relatively long periods without change	Tropical lows very warm. Other lows cold, or warm changing to cold

HOW HIGHS ARE BORN   Local high-pressure areas may develop any place where air cools, compresses, and sinks. Most important in the northern hemisphere are the two large, well-defined high-pressure regions: the horse latitudes and the polar high. In both places, air accumulates, becomes heavy, and settles to earth.

As a mass of air settles over an area favorable for development of a high, it slowly develops into a clockwise-spiraling anticyclone, or high-pressure cell. Air flows from the high-pressure area into the surrounding area of lower pressure. As it pushes out, it is twisted to its right by the earth's rotation. Air moving north shifts to the east; air moving south shifts to the west. The result is the formation of a whirling high-pressure cell. Such cells, forming north of the polar front, repeatedly sweep southward. Highs may extend to Mexico and the Gulf in winter. They are usually several hundred miles in diameter but vary in size. A large high-pressure cell may cover the entire United States east of the Rockies.

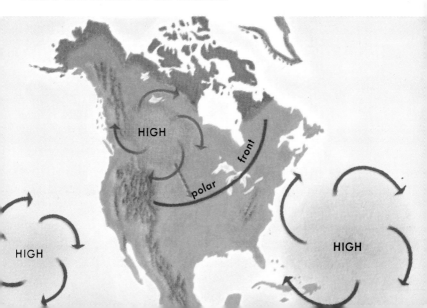

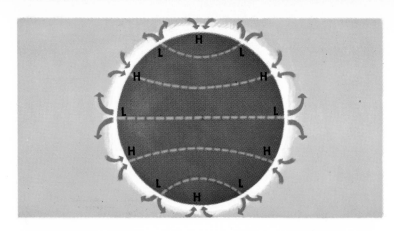

SEASONAL AND GEOGRAPHICAL EFFECTS ON
HIGHS   If the earth were completely covered with water (see above), there would be permanent low-pressure bands at the equator and at about latitude 60° because of the rising air at these places. There would be permanent high-pressure belts of sinking air at the horse latitudes and the poles. But solar radiation heats oceans and land masses differently. This and seasonal heat changes make the actual conditions quite complex. As examples, the coldest region in winter is not over the North Pole but over Siberia, about latitude 70° N. The average temperature of San Francisco in July is lower than at Fairbanks, Alaska. In summer the land is relatively warm and the oceans cool.

Because of these factors, high-pressure zones form in a spotty fashion instead of in wide belts. In the northern hemisphere, they form almost entirely over the cool oceans—particularly in summer, when the land is warm. The maps show this. The two "permanent" highs that cover the eastern parts of both Pacific and Atlantic are the Pacific and Azores anticyclones. But keep in mind that individual highs move with the general circulation of the earth—northeast between latitude 30° and 60°, and southwest between latitude 60° and the pole.

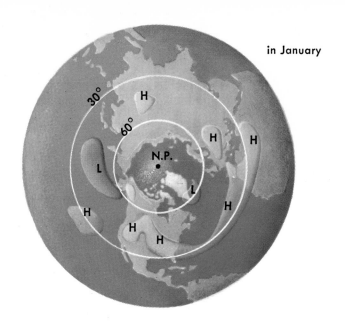

in January

Normal position of highs (H) and
lows (L) in the northern hemisphere

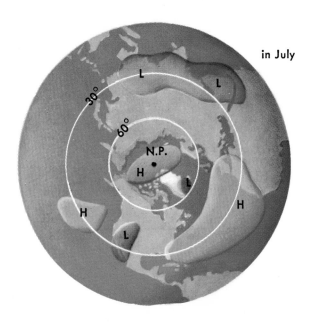

in July

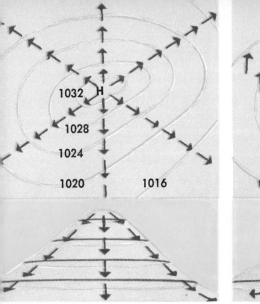
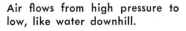
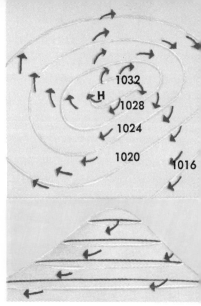

Air flows from high pressure to low, like water downhill.

The earth's rotation makes northern hemisphere air spiral clockwise.

WIND MOVEMENTS WITHIN HIGHS follow a normal flow from high pressure to low pressure, just as water flows down a hill. But the flow is modified by the earth's rotation.

The diagram at left shows the situation that would exist if the earth did not rotate. Note the "isobars" (lines connecting all places of equal pressure), as they appear on weather maps. The numbers refer to air pressure in "millibars" (units of pressure used by meteorologists). The higher the number, the greater the pressure. Standard average sea-level pressure is 1,013 millibars. On a non-rotating earth, winds from a high would move out across the isobars in all directions.

The diagram at right shows how the earth's rotation twists the outflowing air so that winds begin to flow around the isobars as if water were flowing down the sides of a spinning hill. Note the changes in direction as the earth's rotation twists the winds to their right.

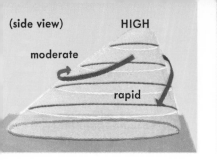

(side view) HIGH moderate rapid

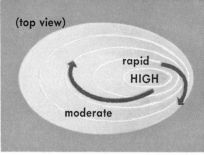

(top view) rapid HIGH moderate

WIND VELOCITIES IN HIGHS Isobars resemble the lines on contour maps. Instead of altitudes, they show pressure intensity. Where isobars are close together, the pressure changes rapidly and winds are fast. Where they are far apart, winds are comparatively slow.

Winds on the ground and winds aloft At about 2,000 ft. above the ground, winds follow isobars closely and do not spiral outward appreciably as they do at the surface; they are governed primarily by the earth's rotation, and are not affected by friction with the ground. But winds on the ground are slowed by surface friction. The earth's rotational effect is reduced, so air continues to spiral out under pressure from the center. The angle at which winds blow across isobars varies from about 10° over ocean to 45° or more over rough land. So winds overhead generally move 45° to the right of their direction on the ground and move about twice as fast.

Winds aloft blow about 45° to the right of those on ground.

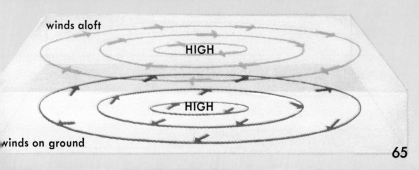

winds aloft HIGH HIGH winds on ground

HIGH

LOW

HOW TO LOCATE HIGHS AND LOWS • Highs generally bring fair weather; lows, poor weather. So it is useful to know whether a high or low is coming your way. This can be done with fair accuracy by the application of a simple rule. Stand with your back to the wind. Turn about 45° to your right; now your back is to the wind as it is blowing well above the ground. The high-pressure center is to your right, the low-pressure center to your left. This rule holds for the northern hemisphere and is quite accurate for general winds. It will not hold for local breezes caused by unequal heating (land and sea breezes, for example). In the southern hemisphere, the directions are reversed: the high pressure is on your left, the low on your right.

Since both highs and lows travel generally in an eastward direction, in the zone of prevailing westerlies, any high or low to your west will likely move over you. But here is where uncertainty enters. Highs and lows may remain stationary, fade out, or move to the north or south. So our rule has but limited usefulness. Once you've mastered the facts about air masses and fronts (pp. 68-94) and learned to read weather maps (pp. 132-141), you can use this general rule more judiciously.

LOWS ARE FORMED by a horizontal wavelike action between two highs of different temperatures (1). The wave gets larger and finally breaks like an ocean wave. The whirling air creates a low-pressure cell. This complicated process which forms major lows is discussed with fronts (pp. 77-94).

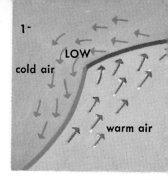

A local low may form when air under a large cumulonimbús cloud is rapidly rising (2). This low-pressure area is filled by surrounding air moving in and twisting counterclockwise because of the earth's rotation. Such cyclones are about 20 miles in diameter.

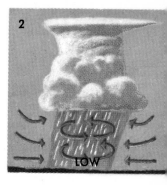

A heat low develops over deserts and other intensely heated places. The hot air expands, rises, and flows outward higher up; thus less air piles up in the area. Pressure drops, and surrounding air rushes in with a swirling motion (3). Such a low lasts most of the summer in southwestern Arizona and southeastern California. Dust devils are small-scale heat lows.

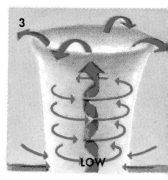

Sometimes lows form on the leeward side of mountain ranges, where they may cause weather disturbances (4). Frequently they form east of the Rockies in Colorado and in the Texas Panhandle.

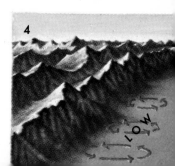

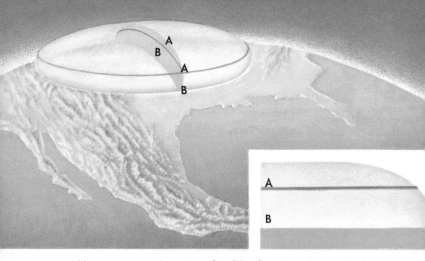

Air mass properties at any level (such as A or B) are similar.

Air Masses

"Air mass," a term in constant use, means "high-pressure cell," but this term carries a different emphasis. An air mass is a vast body of air (often covering hundreds of thousands of square miles) in which the conditions of temperature and moisture are much the same at all points in a horizontal direction. An air mass (anticyclone or high) takes on the temperature and moisture characteristics of the surface over which it forms. For example, an air mass forming over northern Canada and the Arctic in winter is very cold and dry because of the low temperature and humidity there.

The United States is swept by air masses of great contrasts. The North American continent is wide at the top. Cold, dry air masses continually form there and move southward. The southern part of the continent is narrow. The moist, hot tropical air masses which form over the oceans can easily move north. When a hot, moist mass meets a cold, dry mass, a weather "front" (pp. 77-95) usually develops.

AIR MASSES THAT AFFECT OUR WEATHER move across the country and carry with them the temperature and moisture of their origin. An air mass is modified by the surface over which it moves, but its original characteristics tend to persist.

Air masses come from either of two sources: tropical regions or polar regions. On weather charts, tropical air masses are marked T, polar ones P. The two types of surfaces over which these are formed are the continental (c) and oceanic or maritime (m). Polar air formed over oceans is marked mP; polar air formed over land is marked cP. Finally, a third letter is added to indicate whether air is colder (k) or warmer (w) than the surface over which it is moving. So if polar, continental air were moving over ground warmer than itself, it would be marked cPk.

At least three different air-mass classification systems are used by U.S. weather experts, but they need not concern us here. Below are the principal air masses that affect our weather, and their typical paths. Note that the air-mass paths starting in the north are polar (P); those from the south are tropical (T).

Typical paths of air masses over the United States.

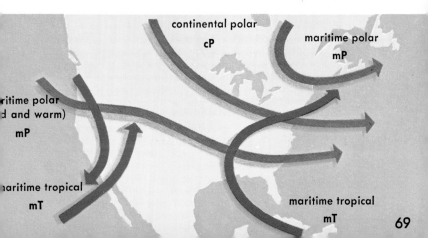

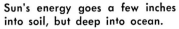

Sun's energy goes a few inches into soil, but deep into ocean.

Heat needed to melt ice delays the seasons over the oceans.

CONTINENTAL AND MARITIME AIR MASSES differ in temperature and humidity, so continental air brings weather very different from maritime air. Land and sea reflect solar radiation differently (p. 7). More heat is needed to raise water temperature than to raise land temperature. Only the top few inches of solid earth absorb radiation, while oceans absorb heat to a depth of 80 ft. or more. Finally, ocean turbulence carries heat even deeper.

The result of all this is that oceans are slower to warm up and to cool than land. Oceans lag behind continents by one or two months in their response to seasonal changes. Furthermore, there is less than 18°F difference between average winter and summer temperature over most open ocean areas! This thermal lag and its moderating effects arise because much spring heat on the ocean is used in melting ice in arctic and antarctic oceans. As much heat is required to melt a pound of ice at 32° to water at 32°F as is required to heat a pound of water from 32° to 176°F. Thus oceans warm slowly in spring and cool slowly in fall because the same great amount of heat is thrown off as arctic water freezes. This heat warms the air and causes a lag in the coming of cold weather. Thus, maritime air tends to moderate extremes of either heat or cold as it moves over the land.

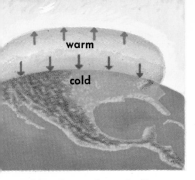
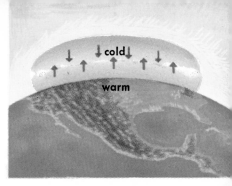

Stable: thermodynamically
warm air mass

Unstable: thermodynamically
cold air mass

STABILITY OF WARM AND COLD AIR MASSES

determines what weather air masses bring. Vertical air currents are created by mountains, or by heating or cooling of air by contact with the surface. Stable air resists these vertical currents and quickly returns to normal. Unstable air allows the vertical currents to grow.

An air mass moving over a surface colder than itself is thermodynamically warm. Such an air mass is stable. An air mass moving over a surface warmer than itself is thermodynamically cold and is generally unstable.

A thermodynamically warm air mass is cooled by contact with the colder earth below. The cooled, heavy, lower surface tends to stay at the bottom. If lifted, it sinks back. But when a thermodynamically cold air mass is warmed by contact with the earth, the warm, light air rises through the cold air above. So a thermodynamically cold air mass is turbulent, with cumulus-type clouds.

IMPORTANT FACTS ABOUT AIR MASSES					
r ss	Stability	Turbulence	Surface visibility	Clouds (if any)	Precipitation (if any)
ld	unstable	turbulent gusty	good	cumulus forms	thunder-showers
rm	stable	steady winds	poor	stratus forms	drizzle

Typical paths of cP air.

Appalachians

Great Lakes

Effect of lakes on cP air.

cP air—cold and clear.

cP air—snow in California.

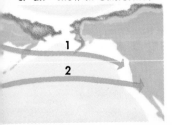

Typical paths of mP air.

WINTER AIR MASSES

Continental Polar (cP) air masses are extremely cold. When traveling over warmer surfaces they are continental polar cold (cPk). These air masses are unstable (p. 71) and flying in the lower levels is turbulent. Their most common path is marked "A" in the map. As cPk air goes over the Great Lakes (particularly before they are frozen), its lower parts are warmed and moistened by the water at about 33° to 38°F. This warmed air rises through colder upper air, causing snow flurries or showers on the leeward side of the lakes. A locality on the eastern shore of the Lakes will have three to five times as much snow in a winter as one on the western shore. Pushed higher over the Appalachians, the cPk air is adiabatically cooled further, and more precipitation results. Hence skies are generally clear east of the Appalachians as the relatively dry air sinks and warms.

Sometimes cP air takes Path B on our map. The air is turbulent; cumulus clouds may form. But the lack of warm lakes and of mountains on Path B means generally clearer skies than when cP air is moving along path A. The third path, C, is rare. On this path, cP air hits the ocean and collects moisture. It brings squalls and even snow as far south as southern California.

Maritime Polar (mP) air may take a relatively short trip over the Pacific (Path 1, at left) before hitting the Coast. Rain or snow showers are common as the air is lifted over coastal ranges. It can also go over the Rockies to stagnate in the Mackenzie valley, becoming cP. If mP air is over the ocean longer (Path 2), it will warm up and get wetter. Such air masses are com-

AIR MASSES

mon on the Pacific Coast in winter. They cool on contact with the land; rain and fog result.

Maritime Polar air rising over the mountains produces clouds and heavy precipitation on windward slopes. It may stagnate between coastal mountains and the Rockies in the Great Basin region. If it goes east over the Rockies, it warms as it descends the east slopes, and brings clear skies, low humidity, and mild weather.

mP air—West Coast fog.

mP—clear east of Rockies.

Maritime Tropical (mT) air is hot and humid at its source. Being hotter than the land surface of the United States, it is stable (mTw). Stratus or stratocumulus clouds often form, mostly during night cooling. These tend to disappear by noon because of warming. Little or no precipitation occurs unless mT air runs into a cold air mass. Then warm, light mT air rises over the cold air and precipitation results. This happens often (p. 86), accounting for more rain in the United States than any other cause. But mT air seldom moves over the north or northeast part of the United States in winter. When it does, the cold land surface may cause extensive fog. It can also cause dense ocean fogs as it crosses the line dividing the Gulf Stream from the cold waters of the North Atlantic.

Maritime Tropical air rarely enters the United States via the Pacific Coast. It does so only when extremely low pressure exists off California. Then the warm, moist mT air moves in and rises rapidly over the heavier, colder air it encounters, or over the Sierra Nevada and other western ranges. In either case, despite its stability, the mT air produces heavy rainfall in southern California.

Typical paths of mT air.

mT air

cold air

mT over cold air—rain.

mT air—rain on mountains.

SUMMER AIR MASSES

Continental Polar (cP) air in summer differs from cP air in winter. The source regions are warmer and the general circulation of the atmosphere is weaker because there is less temperature difference between polar and tropical regions. Air moves slowly over the United States. Fair weather prevails; a few cumulus clouds are produced by local heating. Rains occur over the Great Lakes and in the eastern mountains.

Summer cP air usually brings fair weather.

Pacific Coast mP air in summer produces sea and coastal fogs in California. Moist maritime air passes over a cold ocean surface off the coast. Cooled underneath, the mP air produces dense sea fog, which rolls inland and may hang on for weeks. Farther inland, mP air is warmed quickly by contact with the land; so its relative humidity drops. Although the air is unstable, its humidity is so low that skies remain clear from areas just inside the coastline to the Sierras, on whose west slope showers may fall.

Summer mP air brings fog to the California coast.

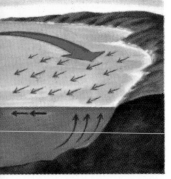

The cold ocean surface that causes West Coast fogs is a result of the "upwelling" of subsurface waters. Friction of the prevailing northwest wind over the Pacific pushes coastal surface waters to its right: that is, toward the southwest. The result: the colder subsurface water rises or wells up. This colder water cools the air above it, producing fog and stratus which may then move in over the coastal region, producing cool weather and interfering with flying.

Cold up-welling off California coast.

Atlantic Coast mP air in summer forms over cold North Atlantic waters. It is colder than the cP or mT air which generally sweeps the eastern states. mP air occasionally flows in over land. When it does, it brings cool weather which sometimes may reach as far south as Florida. If mP makes contact with mT air from the south, frontal weather (typically low stratus clouds and drizzle) occurs as the mT air is lifted and cooled.

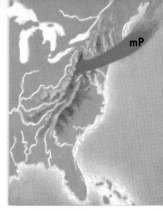

Typical path of Atlantic coast mP air.

Maritime Tropical (mT) air formed over the Pacific is of little importance in summer. It does come inland and may go as far north as Alaska. But it is nearly always mTw, so it is stable and generally brings little disturbance.

Atlantic mT air, on the other hand, is more important in summer than in winter. Central and Eastern states are affected, as is sometimes the Southwest. Atlantic mT air moves almost continuously over the Central and Eastern states in summer, bringing humidity and oppressive heat.

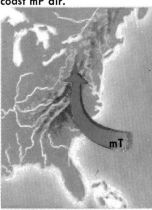

Atlantic mT air brings heat and humidity to the East.

mT air formed in the Caribbean is extremely hot and humid in summer. It is unstable as it comes in over the hotter southern coastal states. As land cools rapidly at night, the air's stability increases and stratocumulus clouds form, with bases near the ground. These clouds usually clear by mid-morning as the land again warms and heats the air. Further heating, later in the day, increases instability again and showers and thunderstorms may result from rapidly rising moist air that cools to below its saturation point.

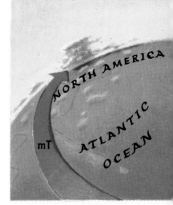

Caribbean mT air brings showers to the South.

Polar air masses may undergo great changes.

POLAR AIR MASSES change rapidly as they sweep over the United States. cP air is initially colder than land over which it travels, so bottom layers are warmed by the earth and rise, creating turbulence, cumulus clouds, and precipitation. The air is further warmed by heat of condensation. Thus polar air tends to mix and get warm. The map shows changes in winter air starting in Siberia as a dry cP air mass. Warmed and moistened by the ocean, it becomes mP air. Cooling by passage over land and mountains causes it to drop its moisture and it continues on as dry, relatively warm air.

TROPICAL AIR MASSES change slowly because they are warmer than land over which they travel. The map shows the path of hot, moist mT air. Bottom layers, cooled by land do not rise—there is no mixing. Further cooling by Eastern mountains or lakes increases stability further. mT air usually remains the same for a long time— hot summer days in the Midwest and East go on and on.

Tropical air masses usually change slightly.

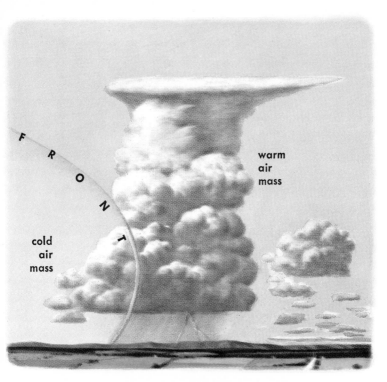

Labels in image: F R O N T, warm air mass, cold air mass

Fronts and Frontal Weather

FRONTS form when air masses collide, for air masses do not mix unless they are very similar in temperature and moisture content. What usually happens is the formation of a boundary, or front. The colder air mass pushes under the warm one and lifts it. Then, if the boundary doesn't move, the front becomes stationary. More commonly it does move, and one air mass pushes the other along. If the cold mass pushes the warm air back, we have a cold front; such a front is pictured above. If the cold air retreats, warm air pushing over it gives us a warm front. In either case, frontal weather is either unsettled or stormy. Fronts usually bring bad weather.

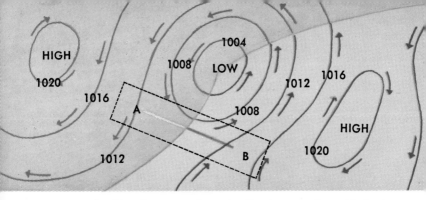

Looking down on a front (outlined area enlarged below).

FRONT FACTS The illustration shows a typical front as seen from above. A warm high is to the right, a cold high at the left. Arrows show the wind directions; isobar lines show pressure in millibars. At the bottom is a block view of the same front. Line A-B has the same position in each diagram. Six facts, true of all fronts, are apparent: (1) Fronts form at margins of high-pressure cells. (2) Fronts form only between cells of different temperatures. (3) Warm air always slopes upward over cold air. (4) A front is found along a low-pressure trough (few exceptions), so pressure drops as the front approaches, rises after it passes. (5) Wind near ground always shifts clockwise (in the northern hemisphere) as the front passes. (6) A front always slopes upward over cold air either ahead of or to the rear of its direction of advance.

Three-dimensional enlargement of area outlined above.

warm high

low-pressure trough

cold high

wind NW

wind SW

A

B

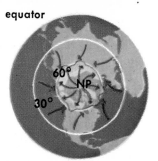 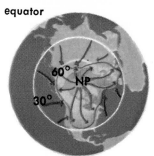

Polar front (dark blue line), shown at left in theoretical position, often breaks through (right). Arrows show wind flow.

POLAR AND EQUATORIAL FRONTS

At latitude 60°, conditions are ideal for a permanent front. Prevailing westerlies from the southwest (red arrows) run into polar easterlies (blue arrows) from the northeast. The polar air is cold, the westerlies relatively warm. But the position of the polar front that forms is not static. Pressure builds up near the pole, and the polar air breaks through to form the masses of cP or mP air that move over North America. Weather, especially in the central and eastern states, is influenced by movements of this polar front.

The so-called equatorial front (intertropical convergence zone) is not a true front, for temperatures to the north and south are about the same. But in late summer the zone moves north. A real line of weather activity may then develop—which accounts in part for hurricanes.

The black line shows the position of the intertropical convergence zone in February (left) and September (right).

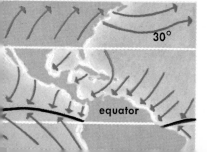 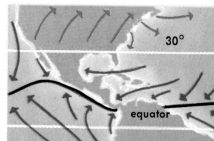

IN WINTER major fronts form and move differently than in summer. The difference is due to the lowering of pressure in summer as continents warm up. Winter fronts move far south; cold polar air pushes to Florida or farther. Strong wind and temperature differences of land and sea push fronts back and forth. The most active fronts of the northern hemisphere form (1) in northwest parts of the Pacific, from Aleutian low-pressure troughs, and (2) in northwest parts of the Atlantic, from the Icelandic low. East of the Rockies, fronts move generally southeastward bringing changing weather.

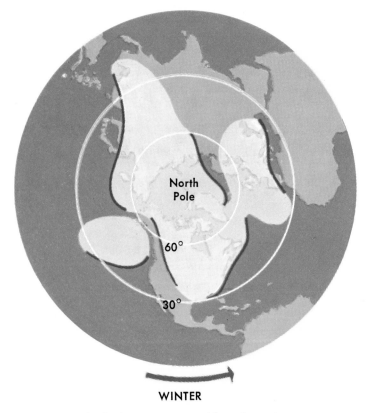

WINTER

Dark blue lines are zones of front formation.

IN SUMMER major fronts in the northern hemisphere form and move like those of winter. But fronts do not move so far south. They are much weaker than winter fronts because of the warming and expansion of the air by the warm continents. Held back by prevailing westerlies, summer fronts do not often bulge down over the southern United States. Maritime tropical air often swells far north, bathing most of the United States in hot, sticky weather. When a front does move south, relief tends to be short-lived, and the front is soon pushed north again by maritime tropical air.

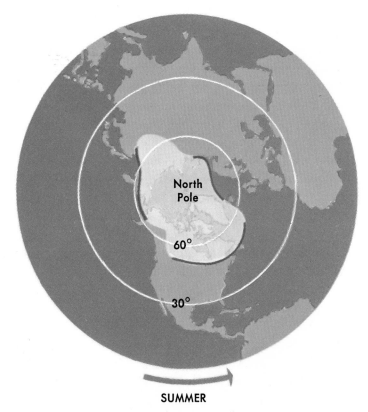

SUMMER

At this time the zones of formation are farther north.

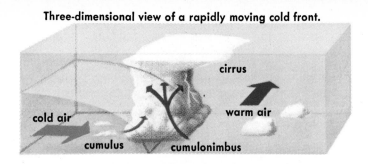

Actual slope of a cold front (blue wedge). Left end of black line i

COLD FRONTS wedge their way under warm air as they advance. The typical thick wedge of a cold front develops as friction with the ground holds back the bottom of the advancing mass of cold air. So the cold air aloft tends to pile into a rounded prow as it advances against warm air. The long wedge diagram above shows the actual slope.

In the northern hemisphere, major cold fronts usually lie in a northeast to southwest direction and move toward the east or southeast. The reason is apparent from the maps on pp. 80-81. Here all cold, polar air is colored blue. As the general movement is east, the cold air masses advance in that direction. Note that cold fronts (easterly edges of cold air masses) are almost always oriented northeast to southwest.

Cold fronts usually advance at speeds of about 20 mph —faster in winter than in summer, because in winter the air is colder and exerts greater pressure.

Although the sloping edge of a cold front may extend over several hundred miles horizontally, the steepness of the advancing edge means that frontal weather is limited to an extremely narrow band (clouds in the drawing above are greatly exaggerated horizontally). The steep sloping edge also produces abrupt lifting of warm air, so that storms at a cold front are generally brief though violent.

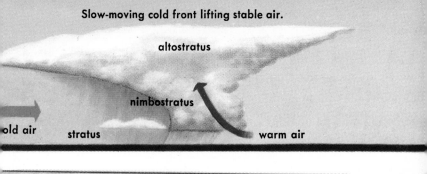

Slow-moving cold front lifting stable air.

altostratus

nimbostratus

old air   stratus   warm air

above ground—front is on surface (right) 100 miles away.

Weather at slowly moving cold fronts differs from weather accompanying rapidly moving fronts. If the warm air is stable, nimbostratus clouds will form almost directly over the front's contact with the ground, and rain will fall through the cold mass after the front has passed. If the cold front is weak, neither rain nor clouds may form.

If unstable and very humid air is pushed over a slowly moving cold front, cumulonimbus clouds will form and thundershowers may fall. But the chief rainfall will be through the cold mass after the front has passed. Typically, a steady downpour from nimbostratus clouds at the lower levels alternates with rain in sheets from cumulonimbus clouds towering above.

Slow-moving cold front lifting unstable air.

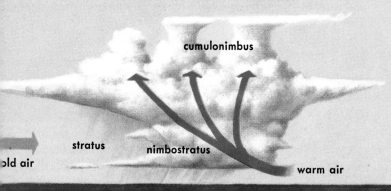

cumulonimbus

stratus   nimbostratus

old air   warm air

SQUALL LINES may precede fast-moving cold fronts. They are an unbroken line of black, ominous clouds, towering 40,000 ft. or more into the sky, including thunderstorms of almost incredible violence and occasional tornadoes. Such squall lines are extremely turbulent, sometimes more so than a typical hurricane. They can tear a light airplane apart and are avoided by all except radar-equipped planes. From the ground, a squall line looks like a wall of rolling, boiling, black fog. Winds shift and sharpen suddenly with the approach of the squall line, and downward-pouring rain may carry the cloud clear to the ground in sharp, vertical bands. Torrential rains fall behind the leading edge of the squall line. Flash floods are common, and dry ravines may become raging torrents within minutes as run-off water rushes through.

Squall lines occur when winds above a cold front, moving in the same direction as the front's advance, prevent the lifting of a warm air mass. This is why little bad weather occurs right at the surface front. But 100 to 150 miles ahead of the front the strong winds force up the warm air with almost explosive violence, producing the squall line.

WEATHER SEQUENCES within a strong cold front are usually the same. First one notices a sharpening of winds from the south or southwest and the appearance of altocumulus clouds darkening the horizon to the west or northwest. The barometer begins to fall.

As the front approaches, the clouds lower and cumulonimbus clouds begin to tower overhead. Rain spatters down, then increases in intensity. The wind may increase and the barometer fall still further.

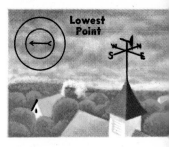

With the actual passage of the front over the observer, the wind shifts rapidly to west or north, blowing in strong gusts. Squall-like rains continue and the barometer hits its lowest reading. Passage of the front usually results in fairly rapid clearing, but in moist or mountainous regions, cumulus or stratocumulus clouds may stay overhead for some time. The barometer rises rapidly; temperature drops. Winds generally become steady from west or northwest.

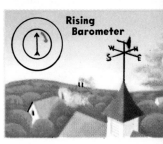

After passage of a cold front we experience for a few days the typical weather of a high (p. 60). Then steadily increasing cloudiness usually indicates an approaching warm front (pp. 86-88).

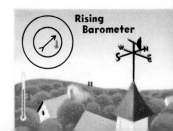

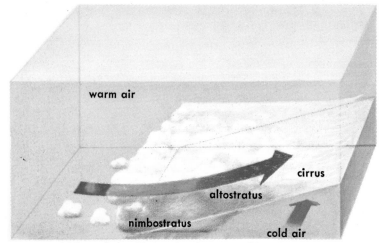

warm air

cirrus

altostratus

nimbostratus

cold air

Warm front. Warm air rides over cold surface air.

WARM FRONTS are those in which warm air advances, replacing colder air. In the Northern Hemisphere, warm fronts occur on the east side of low-pressure cells and are usually followed by cold fronts as the prevailing westerlies move the low eastward (p. 90).

The advance of warm fronts, horizontally, is usually at about 15 mph or slower—that is, about half the speed of cold fronts. The vertical slope between warm and cold air in a warm front is much less steep than in a cold front. The warm air moves gradually up the slope, without the typical cold-front bulge. This is because ground friction drags the bottom edge of the retreating cold air into a thin wedge.

Warm-front weather extends over an area hundreds of miles in advance of the front line at ground level. Typical cloud sequences may be noted 1,000 miles in advance of the front, and often 48 hours in advance of its arrival. The clouds and precipitation typical of warm fronts develop along the contact zone of the warm and cold air above the ground, as shown above.

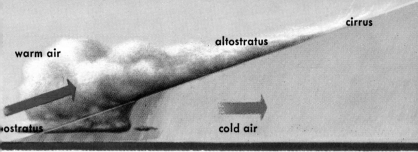

Warm front. Clouds of the stratus type form as stable warm air climbs up a slope of cold air.

Stable warm air, lifted over cold air as a warm front advances, produces stratus-type clouds because the up-lift of air is slow and little turbulence results in the stable air. As the air lifts (see p. 88 for sequence observed from the ground), it cools to produce stratus, nimbostratus, alto-stratus, cirrostratus, and cirrus clouds in that order. Pre-cipitation is heavy at the beginning of the lift, but decreases gradually, leaving relatively dry cirrus clouds at 20,000 ft. or higher.

Unstable warm air produces more violent weather. Turbulence is high, and the unstable air sets up ascend-ing air currents creating cumulonimbus clouds and thun-derstorms ahead of the front line. The precipitation is therefore spotty, alternating between heavy downpour and slow drizzle, with thunderstorms interspersed.

Cumulonimbus forming as unstable warm air rises up slope of cold air.

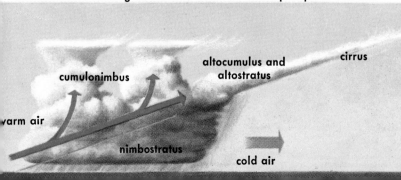

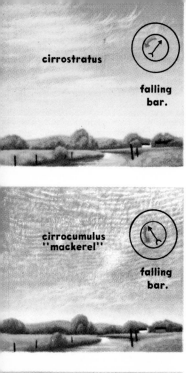

cirrostratus

falling bar.

cirrocumulus "mackerel"

falling bar.

altostratus

falling bar.

cumulus

rising bar.

WARM-FRONT WEATHER SEQUENCE first displays cirrus clouds, which have been lifted farthest up the cold-air slope. These change into cirrostratus, and become denser as the front advances. (Circles represent barometer with black arrow as the needle, and red arrow showing whether pressure readings are rising or falling.)

If cirrocumulus clouds ("mackerel sky") appear, the warm air overhead is unstable and weather described at the bottom of p. 87 is almost certain to come, as old-time sailors and farmers knew.

If the warm air overhead is stable, cirrus clouds are replaced by middle-height altostratus (leaden sky). Unstable cirrocumulus are also replaced by altostratus. Rain or snow begins as the altostratus becomes dense, and continues until the front has passed.

Stratocumulus, nimbostratus, stratus, and—in unstable air—cumulonimbus clouds finish the warm-front sequence. But rain falling through cold air adds to its moisture content, producing lower stratus clouds that often obscure higher clouds. The skies clear as the front passes.

STATIONARY FRONTS are those which move little or not at all. Conditions are much like those accompanying a warm front, but are usually more mild. Stationary fronts with rain may hang on for days.

WEAK FRONTS often pass unnoticed except by weather men. Occurring when air masses are almost identical in humidity and temperature, they are marked only by a wind shift as the weak front passes. Weather men watch weak fronts for possible regeneration into strong fronts.

WEST

EAST

front

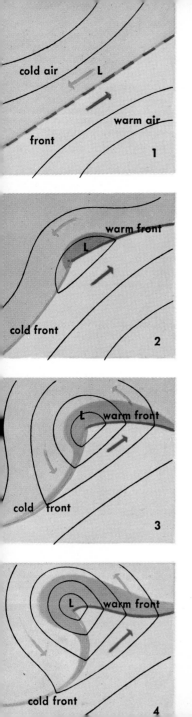

cold air   L

warm air

front

1

warm front

L

cold front

2

L   warm front

cold front

3

L   warm front

cold front

4

LIFE HISTORY OF A FRONTAL LOW

Fronts tend to move across the United States in a generally east or southeast direction. Warm fronts are usually followed closely by cold fronts. To understand why, observe the way "extratropical" low-pressure cells develop from wavelike outbreaks along frontal lines. The pictures show the development of a typical low as it might be seen from above. Black lines are isobars. Purple areas mark precipitation.

(1) A frontal line exists at a low-pressure trough between cold and warm air masses. (2) Cold air begins to push under the warm air at some point, forming a wavelike pattern at the front. (3) The cold front continues to push back the warm air and go under it. Warm air, pushed from one side, bulges out at its front into a low-pressure area, which increases in size as cold air moves away from it. So the warm front advances, adding to the developing wave. (4) The cold front plunges ahead about twice as fast as the warm front. The low pressure area expands as warm air is forced over the low, and the wave forms a distinct crest. (5) The cold front

finally overtakes the warm front, lifting the warm air completely off the ground. (6) Only the low-pressure cell of counterclockwise-swirling air remains near the surface. The swirling low-pressure cell finally disappears as air pressure equalizes. The new front line is established at the boundaries of the cold and warm air masses.

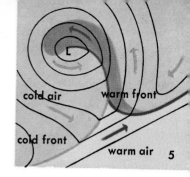

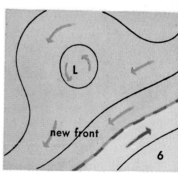

The development and disappearance of a low-pressure cell does not take place in a stationary position. Westerly winds move the air masses from southwest to northeast. So, as a low develops and a cold air mass bends around the tongue of the warm air mass, a warm front moves across the country, followed closely by a cold front. Lowering air pressure and a rapidly dropping barometer precede the warm front with its stormy or generally bad weather. This is followed by the higher pressure of the warm air mass, and a short period of clear weather may result. But the advancing cold front is not far behind. Thus warm fronts, closely followed by cold fronts, move endlessly over the United States.

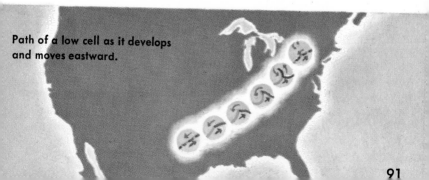

Path of a low cell as it develops and moves eastward.

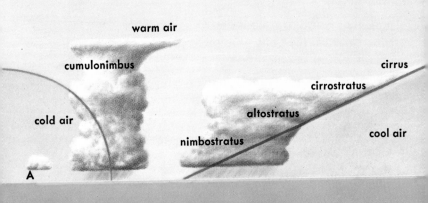

Cold front approaching a warm front prior to occlusion.

OCCLUDED FRONTS The next-to-last position shown for the low on p. 91 marks the development of what is called an "occluded front." This occurs when a cold front, closely following a warm front, finally overtakes the warm front and lifts the warm air mass off the ground. Either the warm front (p. 93, top) or the cold front goes aloft. The top drawings on these two pages show two stages in an occlusion as seen in a side view.

Study these and the diagram of the occluded front as seen from above (lower position, next page). In it, the purple line marks the occlusion. The yellow line (A-B) shows the situation when the cold front has not quite caught up with the warm front. Conditions on the ground in this area are shown in the picture directly above. Warm-front weather is quickly followed by cold-front conditions. The reddish-brown line (C-D) is lying across the occlusion itself; the picture at the top of p. 93 shows conditions on the ground. This is a low-pressure area; surrounding air flows in, equalizing the pressure.

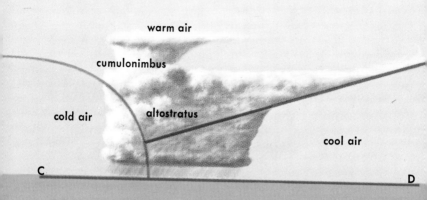

warm air

cumulonimbus

cold air

altostratus

cool air

C

D

Occlusion occurs (above) as the cold front overtakes the warm front and lifts both it and the air mass off the ground.

Below: diagram of the occlusion as seen from above.

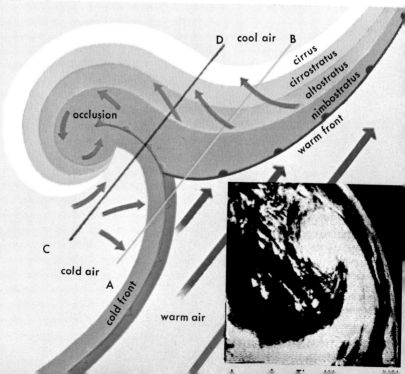

D   cool air   B

cirrus

cirrostratus

altostratus

nimbostratus

warm front

occlusion

C

cold air

A

cold front

warm air

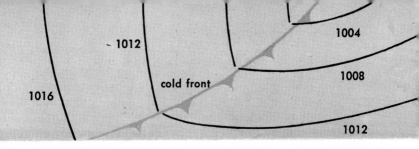

HOW FRONTS ARE SHOWN ON WEATHER MAPS

Most weather changes are brought by fronts. By checking them in newspaper weather maps, you can judge the kind of weather that is approaching and when it will arrive. Keep in mind that weather in the United States moves generally from southwest to northeast. Cold fronts move on the average about 20 mph, warm fronts 15 mph. Cold fronts are indicated on maps by blue lines or lines with peaks (on the side of the line toward which the front is advancing). Warm fronts are shown by red lines or lines with rounded bumps (on the side of the line of advance). Stationary fronts are shown by alternating colors or with peaks and bumps on opposite sides of the line. Occluded fronts are shown by purple lines or alternating peaks and bumps, both on the same side of the line.

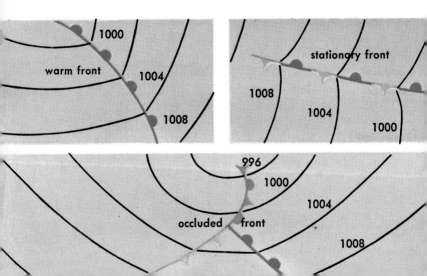

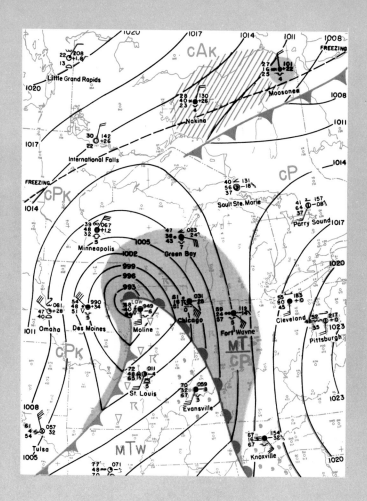

FRONTS AND FRONTAL WEATHER show prominently on weather maps. Above is a wave (p. 90) with both a warm and a cold front. Areas of steady precipitation are marked in solid green; intermittent precipitation in hatched green. Note the symbols for showers ▽ and thunderstorms ⃧ ; also the air mass classification in red and blue.

95

60,000 ft.

Storms

Storms are the most dramatic, most dangerous, and most feared of all weather phenomena. In addition to frontal storms, three other well-known types occur—thunderstorms, tornadoes, and hurricanes.

THUNDERSTORMS represent violent vertical movements of air. They occur as a result of strong uplifting, sometimes building the clouds to heights in excess of 75,000 ft. This uplifting may be due to heating of air by the ground surface (common in the Midwest and East); the action of a cold front; or to temperature differences between land and ocean (common in Florida and the Southeast states).

The map below shows that thunderstorms are most frequent in Florida, the Southeast, the southern Rockies, and adjacent Great Plains. They occur chiefly in summer. Thunderstorms seldom occur on the West Coast, where water-land contrasts in temperature are lowest. Cumulus clouds represent updrafts; cumulonimbus (thunderstorm) clouds have both updrafts and downdrafts. Hurricanes (pp. 104-111) are, in early stages, like giant thunderstorms—with violent updrafts and downdrafts.

JUDGE THE DISTANCE OF A THUNDERSTORM from the fact that light travels at about 186,000 miles per sec. and sound at about 1,100 ft. per sec. or 1 mile in a little less than 5 sec. Judge the distance of a storm by timing how long it takes for thunder to reach you after you see the lightning flash. Counting "1001, 1002, 1003," etc. at a normal speed counts seconds for you. Another aid is to note that cold air, carried down from the thunderhead by rain, may flow forward about 3 miles in front of the storm. So a thunderstorm generally announces its approach by a rush of cold air that flows down and out over the ground ahead of the storm itself.

THUNDERSTORM DISTRIBUTION

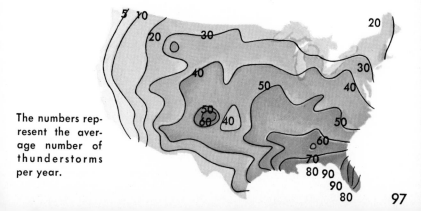

The numbers represent the average number of thunderstorms per year.

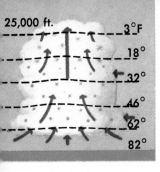

25,000 ft.   3°F
18°
32°
46°
62°
82°

•ı = rain   ✳ = snow

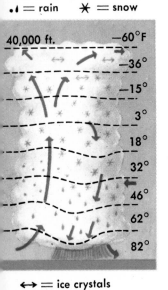

40,000 ft.   −60°F
−36°
−15°
3°
18°
32°
46°
62°
82°

↔ = ice crystals

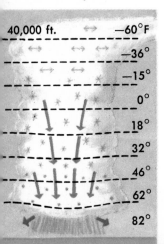

40,000 ft.   −60°F
−36°
−15°
0°
18°
32°
46°
62°
82°

THUNDERSTORM DEVELOPMENT takes place in three recognizable stages.

The cumulus stage is the first stage that each of the many cells of a thunderstorm undergoes. A cumulus cloud develops into a thunderhead when air currents in it extend to about 25,000 ft.

The mature stage begins when ascending air reaches such a height that precipitation occurs (p. 23). In the earlier stage, air in the cloud had been warmer than the surrounding air. But now falling rain and ice crystals cool the air and downdrafts are created. Note how the dotted lines of equal temperature dip with the downdraft.

The final stage occurs when downdraft areas have increased until the entire cloud is nothing but sinking air being adiabatically warmed. As no air is ascending and cooling, precipitation becomes light, then ceases. Steady upper air winds blow the cloud of ice crystals at the top of thunderheads into the typical anvil top.

LIGHTNING is caused by the attraction of unlike electrical charges within a thundercloud, or between it and the earth. The earth normally has a negative charge (a surplus of electrons as compared to atmosphere). Friction of rapidly moving ice particles and rain in a thundercloud "wipes off" electrons and builds up strong electrical charges.

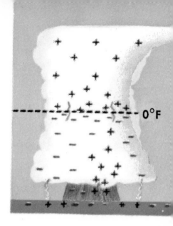

Negative charges (shown here by minus signs) concentrate between the 32°F and 0°F levels. The lower part of the cloud has positive (+) zones surrounded by negative zones. When electrical pressure becomes high enough, charges between parts of cloud or between cloud and earth are released by lightning. First strokes are within the cloud; 65 per cent of all discharges are there or between clouds. Lightning to the ground starts with a relatively thin "leader" stroke from the cloud, followed immediately by a heavy return stroke from the ground.

A single lightning discharge strikes back and forth many times in less than 1/10 second. Most leaders start from the cloud, some from the ground. A lightning discharge is incredibly powerful—up to 30 million volts at 100,000 amperes—but is of very short duration; hence lightning cannot be harnessed or used. But the total energy of a major thunderstorm far exceeds that of an atomic bomb.

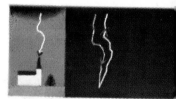

Most leaders start from clouds; some from ground.

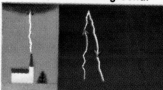

The sudden tremendous heat from lightning causes the compression or shock waves that we call thunder.

99

Danger spots in a storm

Car body shields occupants

Airplane passengers are safe

antenna grounded   antenna not grounded

LIGHTNING SAFETY Lightning strikes thousands of times in the United States each year. Damage runs into the millions, and about 210 people are killed. But if a few elementary precautions are taken, the chances of being hit are exceedingly small. Lightning takes the path of least resistance. It tends to hit the highest places. Never stand under a lone tree in an open field, or fix your TV antenna, during a thunderstorm. The mast of a sailboat may attract lightning. Stay away from boats and water during storms.

Inside your car or in a steel-frame building you'll always be safe. Metal aircraft have often been hit by lightning but seldom with harm to occupants, even though there is often extensive damage to the radio equipment of the plane. The metal skin may be pitted with holes from lightning strikes. On buildings, lightning rods allow electrons to stream off into the air or down into the ground and so tend to prevent strikes. If struck, rods conduct electricity harmlessly to the ground. TV antennas, properly grounded, serve the same purpose. Wood structures and trees have high electrical resistance and are heavily damaged unless grounded.

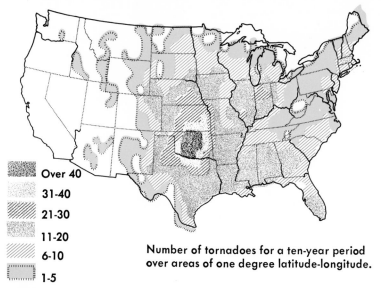

Over 40
31-40
21-30
11-20
6-10
1-5

Number of tornadoes for a ten-year period over areas of one degree latitude-longitude.

TORNADOES are by far the most violent of storms. They are whirlpools of air of such violence that houses in their path may fly apart like matchsticks and even railroad trains may be lifted from their tracks. Fortunately, tornadoes (miscalled cyclones in the Midwest) are of small diameter. Their path of destruction rarely extends ⅛ mile to either side of the dipping, twisting, funnel-shaped cloud which marks the vortex.

An average of 124 tornadoes hit the United States each year, and the great majority of these strike in the lower Mississippi Valley. They result from almost explosive instability in the air, and they accompany heavy thunderstorms and unusually heavy rains—conditions typical of strong cold fronts and squall lines (p. 84). In a study of 92 tornadoes, 72 were found to precede the cold front at an average distance of 165 miles. Tornadoes are easily identified by characteristic radar echoes, and the National Weather Service radar network has become the most effective tool in the issuance of warnings and alerts.

Mammatocumulus clouds form.

Funnel forms as tornado develops.

DEVELOPMENT OF A TORNADO is shown in four stages. Destructive effects do not come from the forward speed of the storm (20 to 40 mph) but from the whirling winds which, near the vortex, often exceed 300 mph. Tornado winds, the strongest known, may have a force 900 times that of a 10-mile breeze and cause unbelievable damage. Extreme low pressure in the vortex causes closed houses or barns literally to explode from the normal pressure of air trapped inside as air pressure drops drastically in the vortex.

Funnel starts its destructive course.

Funnel sucks up dust and debris.

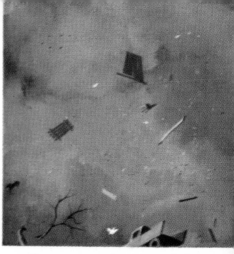

ado can drive straw into tree.   Pressure causes barn to explode.

Another destructive force is a 100- to 200-mph updraft at the center of the funnel. This updraft has sucked houses, animals, and cars into the air and carried them hundreds of feet; it results from the sudden setting off of the explosively unstable air. Tornados have lifted frogs and fish from ponds, then dropped them over populated areas. Red clay when so lifted, mixed with rain, and dropped to earth has been called "a rain of blood." Over lakes and seas the tornado funnel sometimes lifts water into the air, creating a waterspout.

Tornado may "rain" frogs.   Waterspout: tornado over ocean.

103

The eye of hurricane Gloria seen from an airplane.

HURRICANES (OR "TYPHOONS") are tropical cyclones. Like all cyclones they are lows. In some ways they are like the "extratropical" cyclones that exist as low-pressure cells along fronts (p. 90). But hurricanes (with winds of 75 mph or more) are not accompanied by fronts and they differ from frontal "extratropical" lows in important ways. Far more intense than extratropical lows, hurricanes often have winds of over 150 mph. They are about one-third as large, averaging 400 miles in diameter. They move slowly, traveling in an air mass of uniform temperature rather than between air masses of different temperatures. Hurricanes are amazingly symmetrical, the central isobars forming almost perfect circles. Hurricanes develop only over open ocean areas covered by extremely warm moist air masses. They break up soon after moving over land. An interesting difference between hurricanes and extratropical cyclones is the calm "eye" found in the center of the hurricane (p. 108).

Hurricanes generally form in the areas shown in dark blue and travel in the direction of the red arrows.

SOURCES AND PATHS OF HURRICANES   The southwestern part of the North Pacific has more hurricanes (there known as "typhoons") than any other place on earth. These are born between the Marshall Islands and the Philippines, and move in a clockwise fashion, first westward toward the China coast, then northward and northeast over the Philippines toward Korea and Japan.

Ranking second are the hurricanes ("cyclones") of the South Indian Ocean. Some ("Willy-Willies") develop north of Australia and curve down over the northwest coast. More frequent and intense are those that sweep westward, some brushing Madagascar and Southeast Africa.

Third in frequency are the hurricanes that move over the West Indies. These storms, most of which originate near the bulging west coast of Africa, cause great damage to shipping and to the many islands in their path. These are the storms that hit the south and east coasts of the United States or strike Mexico or Central America.

Of eight regions of occurrence, only two, the West Indies and the Mexican West Coast, give rise to hurricanes that affect the United States. The latter seldom strike the continent as far north as California. The map shows the eight sources (dark blue) and paths (red arrows) of hurricanes of the world.

THE BIRTH OF HURRICANES often occurs in regions of contrasting winds, similar to those at fronts. These are near, but not at, the equator, where trade winds meet to form the intertropical convergence zone (ITCZ). But tropical cyclones have never occurred at the equator itself! This is because cyclones require the twisting forces of the earth's rotation to start them spinning (pp. 53-54), and there is none at the equator. Since the ITCZ moves north of the equator in summer to areas where the winds are twisted to their right, cyclonic swirls can be established. And so begins the season of hurricanes that affect the United States.

Another way hurricanes form is by the intensification of a wave or ripple in the easterly trade winds. These easterly waves are watched, and when a ship reports strong wind speeds in its vicinity, reconnaissance aircraft are sent to look over the suspected area.

In winter, when the ITCZ in the Atlantic Ocean is at the equator, hurricanes never develop on it. However, when the zone moves south of the equator in the Indian Ocean and in part of the South Pacific in winter, the season of hurricanes affecting the southern hemisphere begins. Compare the maps (p. 79) showing the February and September positions of the ITCZ with the table of Atlantic hurricanes (below).

TOTAL ATLANTIC HURRICANES BY MONTH OVER A 58-YEAR PERIOD					
Jan.	1	May	1	Sept.	104
Feb.	0	June	14	Oct.	48
Mar.	1	July	15	Nov.	12
Apr.	0	Aug.	64	Dec.	1

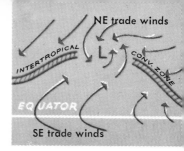

Opposing winds make air whirl.

A hurricane is born in a hot moist air mass over the ocean. The cyclonic motion is often started as opposing trade winds whirl around each other. This can occur only when the ITCZ is displaced from the equator so that the twisting effect of earth's rotation can take place. The rotating low pushes air toward its center, forcing hot moist air there to lift. Lifting causes moisture to condense. Heat thrown off as the moisture condenses (p. 13) further warms rotating air, which becomes even lighter and rises more swiftly. As more and more moist tropical sea air sweeps in to replace the rising air, more and more condensation takes place. So air inside the storm rises faster and faster.

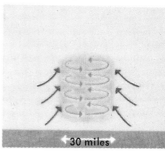

Heat of condensation lifts mass.

Hurricanes are so violent because of the tremendous energy released by the continuous condensation. At first the storm is like the inside of a giant thunderstorm. Unlike a thunderstorm over land, a hurricane has an inexhaustible source of moisture. The heat given off by condensation causes the air in the hurricane to rise faster and faster. Surrounding air sweeps in rapidly until the hurricane is a giant wheel of violent winds.

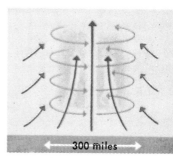

Rise accelerates like a balloon.

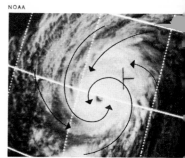

Column is fed from sides.

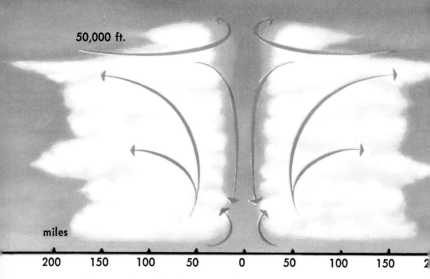

50,000 ft.

miles

| 200 | 150 | 100 | 50 | 0 | 50 | 100 | 150 | 2 |

Section through a hurricane, showing eye and vertical winds.

THE EYE OF A HURRICANE is at the center of the storm—a zone of near calm or light breezes, with clear or lightly clouded skies overhead. It averages about 20 miles in diameter. Thousands, ignorant of the hurricane's anatomy, have gone out into the calm of the eye, unaware that they would soon be hit again by the full might of the other side of the hurricane.

The eye may be caused by centrifugal force acting on winds at the rim of the eye. The centrifugal force acting on a rotating body doubles when the radius of rotation is cut in half. As air spirals in toward the center of a hurricane, its centrifugal force increases greatly. The cloudy wall of the eye is where the centrifugal force exactly balances the pressure forcing air inward to the low-pressure center. Friction with the ocean surface slows down the whirling air and decreases the centrifugal force. So the eye is small at the surface. Aloft, where wind speeds are great, the centrifugal force is higher and the eye larger and funnel-shaped.

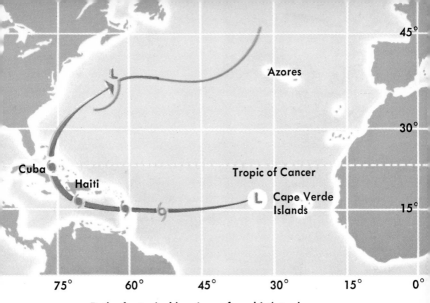

Path of a typical hurricane from birth to decay.

THE LIFE HISTORY OF A HURRICANE can be traced from its birth as a tropical low, through maturity and to decay as an extratropical cyclone in the westerlies. The map above shows a storm starting west of the Cape Verde Islands as a tropical low with winds less than 32 mph. Next we find tropical storm "Betty" (hurricanes are given women's names) with winds 32 to 73 mph, approaching the Leeward Islands of the West Indies. When next reported it is a mature hurricane with winds over 75 mph, right over Guadeloupe. It continues westward at 10 to 12 mph, passing south of Puerto Rico and Haiti. Then it begins to curve north, still at 10 to 12 mph, passing over Cuba and the Bahamas, but now with winds over 125 mph. Betty then curves to the northeast, moving at 30 mph until it hits a cold front north of Bermuda. Hurricane Betty induces a wave on the front and becomes an extratropical low, ending as a storm over the North Sea. Hurricane Betty's path is typical. It could have continued west to hit the Gulf Coast, Florida, or the Atlantic seaboard.

109

Wind blows boats ashore.

Waves undermine buildings.

DESTRUCTIVENESS OF HURRICANES is due to winds up to 200 mph, storm waves and tides, and flash floods caused by torrential rains filling rivers till they overflow as the storm moves inland.

On the average the United States is hit by hurricanes about twice a year. About once every three years an unusually severe hurricane strikes, leaving a swath of destruction 50 to 100 miles wide and sometimes hundreds of miles long.

The violent winds uproot trees, splinter frame buildings, sink or damage ships, and in combination with the high tides erode beaches and wash away shore installations.

The storm tides with the September 8, 1900, hurricane at Galveston, Texas, completely flooded the city. More than 6,000 died and property damage was well over $20,000,000.

Flash floods caused the chief destruction and greatest number of deaths from the 1955 hurricanes that hit the eastern seaboard and New England.

Floods destroy homes.

Hurricane's eye from the cockpit of a reconnaissance plane.

OUR HURRICANE WARNING SYSTEM was established in 1938 by joint action of the U.S. Weather Bureau, Air Force, and the Navy. Previously, hurricanes had struck with little or no warning. Now reconnaissance aircraft, fully equipped with radar scopes and weather instruments, are sent to reconnoiter suspected areas. When a hurricane is spotted, planes fly into the hurricane once every 6 hours to measure the intensity of the winds and exactly locate the center. Bulletins every 6 hours forecast the probable path of the hurricane and give warning. People have time to board up their homes or go to safer places. Ships at sea generally change course to avoid the storm, and aircraft are flown to safe spots away from the coast. Flying into the eye of a hurricane, though extremely rough, is not so dangerous as one might think. Despite the thousands of flights made since the beginning of the program, only three reconnaissance aircraft have been lost in the period between 1938 and 1957.

The microseismograph is a relatively new instrument that picks up disturbances caused by storms at sea. This ultra-sensitive earthquake recorder detects hurricanes earlier so that they can be located and tracked by reconnaissance planes.

Weather Forecasting

Accurate weather forecasting depends on the forecaster's knowing as much as possible about the total state of the atmosphere. The National Weather Service operates a far-flung network of stations where such information is collected and speedily sent to regional forecasting centers. Observations are taken hourly, day and night, at some 400 stations along the U.S. airways. More complete observations are made every 6 hours at many of the stations. Upper air elements are sampled by radiosonde twice daily at some 50 stations. Pilot balloons, measuring the upper air winds, are sent up four times a day at some 125 stations. The Coast Guard, Air Force, Navy, and Federal

The United States is covered by a dense network of stations that report the weather for aviation needs. New York City and Los Angeles are each surrounded by a dozen stations close at hand.

Aviation Administration cooperate in observing and forecasting the weather. Over 9,000 part-time weather stations also report to the National Weather Service.

Weather affecting the United States a week or more from now is being born today in air masses over other countries and the oceans. A world-wide network of weather stations (under the World Meteorological Organization, an agency of the United Nations) exchanges data with the National Weather Service. Merchant ships radio information four to eight times a day while at sea, and airliners report weather conditions encountered in flight. Because of all this, the National Weather Service is able to achieve better than 85 per cent accuracy in its 24-hour to 36-hour forecasts.

The stations on this map are those that report upper-air data. They all explore winds aloft by sending up pilot balloons. Those marked by a triangle report, in addition, data obtained by radiosonde.

Colder; Snow?

For Jefferson County: Colder and increasing cloudiness tonight. Wednesday scattered light rain or snow flurries and colder. Low tonight around 40: High Wednesday in the 40s. Low Wednesday night low 30s.

FIVE-DAY FORECAST
Temperatures will average 4 to 7 degrees below normal. Normal maximum 54 north to 63 south; normal minimum 34 north to 40 south. Colder tonight, Wednesday and Thursday followed by warming trend over weekend. Precipitation total .50 to 1 inches; rain south and rain or snow north Wednesday and again near week end.

Detailed 24-hour and general five-day forecasts.

DUTIES OF THE NATIONAL WEATHER SERVICE include 24-hour detailed forecasts, general 5-day forecasts, 30-day general outlook, 12-hour aviation forecasts (with an accuracy of 85 per cent), reports of weather conditions at over 300 airports, and special bulletins, weather maps, and reports of temperature and precipitation. They issue warnings on storms, frost, etc. for farming and industry. The 24-hour and 5-day forecasts go by radio or teletype. Newspapers and TV broadcasters use the Weather Service's weather maps to prepare their simplified maps.

Before taking off, pilots read reports and forecasts received by teletypewriter in the weather briefing rooms.

```
DEN  15⨀E35⦵100⊕20 217/65/50/0710/031
AKO  E40⦵180⊕15 224/63/55/0710/029/BINOVC NW
GLD  20⨀E120⊕15 220/64/59/0907/026
GCK  20⨀E70⊕15 190/70/60/0520/017
DDC  90⨀E120⊕15R- 166/67/64/0218/009
HLC  E100⨀250⊕15 203/68/58/0214/017
RSL  40⨀150⨀E200⦵15 193/70/59/0410
HUT  50⨀250-⦵15 74/0223G28/003
SLN  E20⦵120⊕15 180/74/61/0216/008
ICT  65⨀E250⊕15 147/77/63/3622/999/TWRG CU SE
TOP  20⨀E80⦵15 169/73/65/3610/004
MKC  M25⦵120⊕15 164/76/65/3620/002
STJ  22⨀E80⊕15 72/65/3612/003/⦵V⦵ BINOVC NW
OFK  250-⦵15 227/62/46/3613
```

A Teletype weather report for pilots.

For air safety, major airports have stations operated by the Federal Aviation Administration or National Weather Service to give pilots complete information. Teletype reports like that shown at the top of the page and decoded at the bottom are available. While in flight the pilot receives weather reports and forecasts every half hour, and can request information at any time. The growth of private and commercial aviation has been paced by the growth of the National Weather Service, which has made safe flying possible.

Following is an interpretation of the fifth line of the Teletype at the top of the page:

DDC   Reporting station Dodge City, Kans.
90 ⨀   Scattered clouds at 9000 ft.
E120 ⊕   Cloud ceiling at an estimated height of 12,000 ft.
15   Visibility 15 miles
R-   Weather: light rain
166   Barometric pressure: 1016.6 millibars
67   Temperature in degrees Fahrenheit
64   Dew point in degrees Fahrenheit
↓↙18   Wind: north-northeast at 0218 miles per hour
009   Altimeter setting of 30.09 inches

LATE CITY EDITION
Condensation of
National Weather Service Forecast
Rain and cooler today; clearing and colder tonight. Fair, cold tomorrow.
Temperature range today : 48-41
Temperature range yesterday : 49.6-40.2

Not a coincidence. Large stores retain private forecasting services to know in advance which merchandise to feature.

PRIVATE AND INDUSTRIAL METEOROLOGISTS supplement the work of government weathermen and supply a great variety of weather forecasting services. If a department store is all set to advertise spring clothes and a consulting forecaster advises that three days of rain and cool weather are ahead, the ads are changed to sell rainwear and cool weather clothing. If a meteorologist employed by a large New York bakery advises that tomorrow's weather will be rainy, the bakery delivers the bulk of its products to downtown stores, knowing that housewives will delay their shopping in the suburbs and call their husbands to "pick up a loaf of bread" near their office. The dairy company makes more ice cream when advised of warm weather. The coat manufacturer makes topcoats instead of overcoats on learning of a mild winter ahead; the rainwear manufacturer makes rubbers instead of boots. The drug manufacturer makes more cold remedies because more people catch colds in the changeable weather of a "mild" winter. Millions of dollars are saved annually through these services.

PRIVATE METEOROLOGY is widespread in today's complex affairs. Some of the larger airlines employ their own meteorologists, who work out complete details of the weather that pilots will encounter on their flights over the U.S. or abroad. Motion picture companies save millions of dollars by arranging their schedule of outdoor shooting on the basis of clear-day predictions of their meteorologists. Some meteorologists have full-time jobs with major utility companies. Their predictions of cool and warm weather and bright and dull days enable the companies to pump gas and generate electricity according to the need.

Private and commercial meteorologists get their basic data from the National Weather Service. This agency makes the observations, draws the maps, and issues the general information from which special forecasts can be made for special purposes. Basic to all forecasting is the collection of data throughout the United States and other parts of the world, the coding of these data for transmission, and the preparation of basic weather maps.

Some airlines have their own staff meteorologists, who help pilots avoid storms by predicting where and when they will occur.

wind
direction
transmitter

remote
recording
anemometer

rain
gauge

sunshine
duration
transmitter

radiosonde
transmitter
and receiver

COLLECTING THE DATA basic to accurate forecasting requires the use of instruments. Until the invention of such instruments, our knowledge of the atmosphere was limited to general ideas distilled from generations of folk wisdom. Farmers, hunters, and sailors were always interested in weather. Their rules of thumb (pp. 142-143) generally held a good deal of truth.

But with the invention of the barometer and thermometer and other measuring instruments, accurate observation was made possible and the science of meteorology was born. The advent of telegraphy and the world-wide standardization of time zones based on Greenwich Civil Time made possible the collection of these data at central points. The next step was analysis and preparation of weather maps for the entire world that showed the conditions of the atmosphere with fair accuracy. It is now possible to prepare weather maps showing simultaneous worldwide conditions every 6 hours of the day and night. Upper-air charts can be prepared every 12 hours.

Details on modern weather instruments follow—but the teletype, radio, and the international cooperation of scientists are essential also.

PRESSURE MEASUREMENTS are essential for the plotting of isobars (lines of equal pressure) over the earth, and for determining positions and movements of fronts. As pressure at mountain tops is less than at sea level, regardless of positions of highs and lows, all pressure readings are converted to what they would be if readings were taken at sea level. This allows accurate mapping of pressure patterns anywhere in the world.

Pressure is measured by two types of barometers. The mercurial barometer is used by most weather stations. It is a glass tube closed at the top and filled with mercury. The mercury column is supported by the pressure of the air, being high in the tube when air pressure is high and lower as air pressure decreases. The reading is converted into millibars.

The aneroid (no fluid) barometer is a corrugated metal container from which the air has been removed. The corrugations and a spring inside prevent air pressure from collapsing it completely. As air pressure increases, the top of the box bends in; as pressure decreases, the top bows out. Gears and levers transmit these changes to a pointer on a dial.

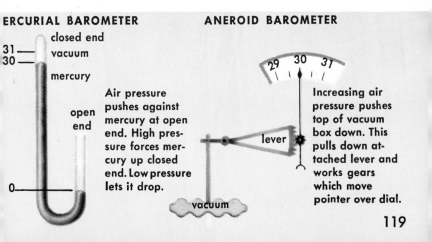

ERCURIAL BAROMETER

closed end
31 —
30 —
vacuum
mercury

open end

Air pressure pushes against mercury at open end. High pressure forces mercury up closed end. Low pressure lets it drop.

0 —

ANEROID BAROMETER

29 30 31

lever

vacuum

Increasing air pressure pushes top of vacuum box down. This pulls down attached lever and works gears which move pointer over dial.

aneroid barometer

recording barometer or barograph

recording barometer or barograph

mercurial barometer

WEATHER STATION MERCURIAL BAROMETERS are precision-made and accurate to 1/1000 inch. They respond to changes in temperature as well as pressure, because the mercury column itself expands with heat. This is corrected by adjusting the level of a pool of mercury at the base of the tube. High accuracy in reading is made possible by a sliding vernier. The observer reads the mercury height along etched lines on the vernier.

Aneroid barometers are not as accurate but have important uses. One, not related to weather, is their use as an altimeter. The dial is marked in feet, and as a pilot flies upward, the pointer gives his altitude above sea level. An aneroid barometer can be arranged also so that changes in pressure are recorded on a paper-covered rotating drum. Most weather stations have such a recording aneroid barometer, or barograph.

TEMPERATURE READINGS

above −38°F are taken with mercurial thermometers (mercury freezes at −38°F). Alcohol thermometers are used below −38°F. (Alcohol freezes at −179°F.) **Minimum thermometers** record lowest temperatures. Surface tension of alcohol keeps a small sliding glass index always at the surface level of the alcohol as it contracts with falling temperature. When the alcohol rises in the tube as temperature goes up, the index remains at the lowest position, indicating the minimum temperature reached. **Maximum thermometers,** like a doctor's thermometer, have a constriction in the mercury tube. As temperature rises, the mercury expands through the constriction. As temperature falls, the constriction keeps the mercury from running back. **A Thermograph,** or recording thermometer, has a Bourdon tube filled with alcohol. It flexes as temperature changes.

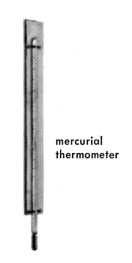

mercurial thermometer

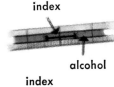

index

alcohol

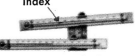

index

Max. and min. thermometer

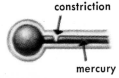

constriction

mercury

thermograph

121

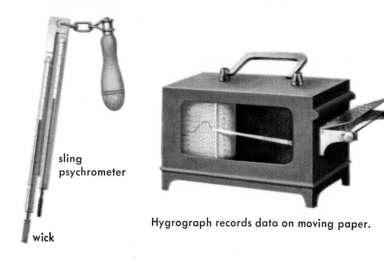

sling
psychrometer

wick

Hygrograph records data on moving paper.

RELATIVE HUMIDITY is measured with a psychrometer, consisting of two thermometers. One is a regular mercury thermometer. The other, a wet bulb thermometer, has a muslin wick over its bulb. The end is dipped into water before a reading is taken. These thermometers are whirled before the psychrometer is read. Evaporation from the muslin wick lowers the temperature of the wet bulb thermometer. In dry air, there is more evaporation and therefore more cooling than in moist air; hence the difference in temperatures shown by the two thermometers indicates the relative humidity (p. 12), which is read from a table. There are several types of psychrometers; they differ mainly in the means for evaporating water from the wet bulb.

Hygrographs are instruments for recording relative humidity. They work like thermographs, except that the humidity element consists of a sheaf of blonde human hairs treated to remove the oil. As the relative humidity increases, the hairs increase in length and operate the recording mechanism. Knowledge of relative humidity is important in predicting precipitation and icing conditions, which can force a plane down.

MEASURING PRECIPITATION is extremely important. The amount of annual rainfall and its seasonal distribution in a locality determine the kinds of farming that are practicable, and may affect the whole pattern of living. The National Weather Service keeps accurate records of precipitation throughout the country.

Rain gauges are of several types and measure not only rain but all other forms of precipitation. Tipping bucket gages have a divided bucket balanced so that one side fills, then tips its water into a container and allows the other side to fill. The gauge is so precisely balanced that 1/100 in. of rain tips the bucket each time. As the bucket tips, it sends an electric signal to a recording drum inside the weather station. Later the station observer measures the water which ran into the container as a check on the recording's accuracy. Another type of recording rain gauge continuously weighs the water and records that weight directly on a graph as inches of rainfall. "One inch of rainfall" is a way of saying that on level ground a layer of rain one inch deep would remain if none of the water ran off or seeped into the ground.

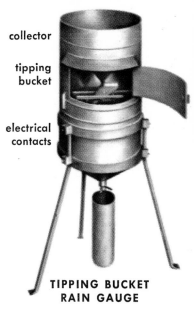

collector

tipping bucket

electrical contacts

TIPPING BUCKET RAIN GAUGE

RECORDING RAIN GAUGE
(housing removed)

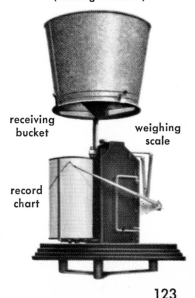

receiving bucket

weighing scale

record chart

123

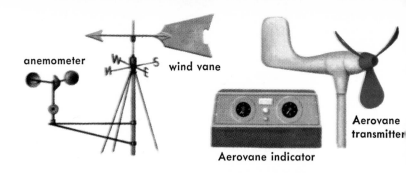

anemometer

wind vane

Aerovane transmitter

Aerovane indicator

WIND SPEED AND WIND DIRECTION INDICATORS

show intensity and direction of air movements. Sudden shifts in wind direction mark the passage of fronts. Precise data on wind direction and speed are determined by a variety of wind vanes and by various types of anemometers, usually recording types which automatically set down a continuous record.

One of the most commonly used instruments is the quadruple recorder, or station meteorograph, which is connected electrically to a wind vane, anemometer, rain gauge, and a device that records sunshine duration. The anemometer part has three cups, which catch the wind and rotate. Gears and electrical connections transmit the wind speed to a dial for direct reading and to the recording graph. The Aerovane is like a small airplane without wings; the nose turns into the wind, showing wind direction, and the whirling propeller gives wind speed in miles per hour.

Accurate information on wind direction and speed helps meteorologists to chart the positions of highs and lows (pressure readings provide the basic data for such charts).

station meteorograph or quadruple recorder

Beaufort Wind Scale In 1805 Admiral Beaufort of the British Navy developed a scale to estimate wind speeds from their effect on the sails. His table is given below, modified for use on land. Beaufort number 3, for example, with winds of 7 to 10 knots (a knot is 1.15 miles per hour), is a gentle breeze that produces constant but light motion of twigs and leaves.

Today, by international agreement, all reports for use in plotting weather maps use knots. Winds are recorded on the weather map to the nearest 5 knots.

ESTIMATING WINDS ON THE BEAUFORT SCALE				
Beaufort number	mph / knots	Description	Observation	Symbols on weather maps
0	0-1 / 0-1	calm	smoke rises vertically	◎ calm
1	1-3 / 1-3	light air	smoke drifts slowly	◎ calm
2	4-7 / 4-6	slight breeze	leaves rustle	5 knots
3	8-12 / 7-10	gentle breeze	leaves and twigs in motion	10 knots
4	13-18 / 11-16	moderate breeze	small branches move	15 knots
5	19-24 / 17-21	fresh breeze	small trees sway	20 knots
6	25-31 / 22-27	strong breeze	large branches sway	25 knots
7	32-38 / 28-33	moderate gale	whole trees in motion	30 knots
8	39-46 / 34-40	fresh gale	twigs break off trees	35 knots
9	47-54 / 41-47	strong gale	branches break	45 knots
10	55-63 / 48-55	whole gale	trees snap and are blown down	50 knots
11	64-72 / 56-63	storm	widespread damage	60 knots
12	73-82 / 64-71	hurricane	extreme damage	70 knots

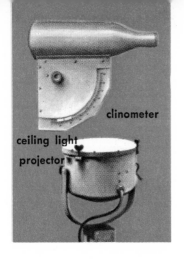

ceiling light projector

clinometer

MEASURING CEILING HEIGHT (the height of the base of clouds that cover more than half of the sky) is important for air safety. Experienced observers can estimate heights to within 100 ft. below 5,000 ft. and to within 1,000 ft. above 5,000 ft.

Ceilings and cloud height also can be measured by balloons and ceilometers. A balloon released from the ground and rising at a fixed rate is timed until it disappears into the cloud. The elapsed time indicates the height of the cloud base.

CEILOMETERS use a detector and a vertical beam of light (ceiling light projector) that makes a bright spot on clouds overhead. The bright spot is observed from 800 to 1,000 ft. away by a man with a clinometer or by a scanning detector. The angle between the horizontal and the line from the detector to the bright spot indicates the height of the clouds. At large airports, a rotating beam ceilometer is used. In this system a light beam rotates vertically through 90° of arc. The bright spot it makes on a cloud is sensed by a detector aimed directly upward. Ceiling heights measured by this system are recorded automatically every 6 seconds and the measurements are more accurate.

Automatic rotating beam ceilometer.

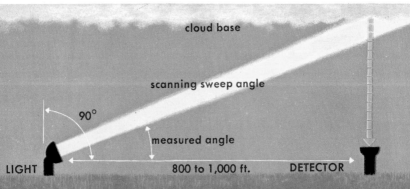

cloud base

scanning sweep angle

90°

measured angle

LIGHT   800 to 1,000 ft.   DETECTOR

SUNSHINE DURATION TRANS-MITTERS are used to record the duration of sunshine each day. This, like the precipitation for a region, is important for agriculture, industry, and resort areas. The transmitter has a "black bulb" containing mercury and a sealed air space above it. When the sun shines, the black bulb is quickly heated and the air expands, pushing mercury

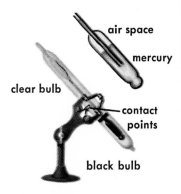

SUNSHINE TRANSMITTER

up the tube and making an electric contact. The resulting electric signal makes a mark on a rotating graph paper. When clouds cover the sun, the bulb cools rapidly and the mercury drops, breaking the electrical contact.

OBSERVING WINDS ALOFT is important to aviation and in preparing upper-level maps for forecasting. These winds are observed either by radar or by use of pilot balloons and a theodolite similar to the surveyor's instrument. Accurate scales measure the angle of the balloon with the ground and its direction from the station. Speed and direction of winds at various levels are easily computed from these observations.

Theodolite and pilot balloon help keep track of winds aloft.

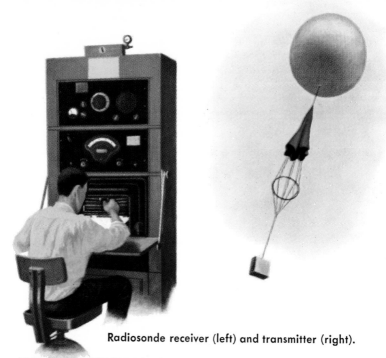

Radiosonde receiver (left) and transmitter (right).

RADIOSONDE MEASUREMENT OF UPPER AIR is one of the more recent and most accurate means of finding the temperature, pressure, and humidity at various heights in the atmosphere. There are several types, but most common is the "modulated audio-frequency system," involving a tiny radio transmitter that broadcasts a special frequency radio wave. Attached to this transmitter is a small but complicated set of measuring instruments which automatically convert data on temperature, pressure, and humidity into electrical impulses, which are sent by the transmitter to a receiving and recording set on the ground.

Radiosondes are sent up on special balloons twice daily by National Weather Service stations. They frequently reach heights of over 100,000 ft. One kind, the dropsonde, is released on a parachute from airplanes flying 20,000 ft. above ocean areas.

On radar, distant storm (left) is overhead 4 hours later (right).

RADAR EQUIPMENT has come into prominent use in weather observation and forecasting work. Designed primarily to track the course of storms (including hurricanes), some forms of radar are carried on airplanes and enable pilots to go around storms or to pick their way through them by avoiding the most turbulent areas (p. 111).

Below is a typical weather station radar equipment set-up. A rotating antenna constantly scans the skies. Radar beams shoot out at the speed of light, are reflected from precipitation cells in clouds, and return to the receiving part of the antenna. The receiver converts the beam to electrical impulses which show up on a screen much as in a television receiver

Screen (left) shows information collected by rotating antenna (right).

NOAA

WEATHER SATELLITES are the newest observation tool of the meteorologist. The first TIROS (*Television and InfraRed Observation Satellite*) was sent into orbit on April 1, 1960.

Since then the TIROS Operation System (TOS) and the Improved TOS satellites replaced TIROS. The newest ITOS satellites (NOAA 1, NOAA 2, etc.) are equipped with radiometers that produce both daytime and nighttime pictures. Other sensors measure temperature and humidity at many heights in the atmosphere between the satellite and the ground; these data are used to obtain soundings (see RADIOSONDE, p. 128). The radiometer data, sent to ground stations by microwave, are processed into pictures showing clouds, cloud heights, land and sea surface temperatures, sea ice, snow fields, and storms. Since clouds outline fronts, the pictures are used to locate fronts in areas where there are few weather stations.

NOAA satellites orbit the Earth at an average height of 900 miles, making a complete circuit every 115 minutes. These satellites "see" the entire Earth three times a day: visible light sensors take daytime "pictures" and infrared sensors take both daytime and nighttime "pictures" by sensing heat emitted by the Earth and clouds. Geostationary satellites that hover 22,300 miles above a point on the equator take pictures like the one on p. 34 every 30 minutes both by day and by night.

Hurricane Ava 1500 miles south-southwest of San Diego, California, June 7, 1973. This picture, taken from 900 miles up, shows the clouds and circulation typical of hurricanes and typhoons (pp. 104-111). The storm is about 400 miles in diameter. The well marked circular eye in the center of the storm is about 20 miles across. Picture constructed from data from daytime scanning radiometer on NOAA 2.

NOAA

Geographical features are often easy to see in satellite photographs. In this photo, the coast of the United States from the Delaware peninsula to southeastern Maine is visible. The bright streak of clouds across the bottom of the picture parallels a jet stream (pp. 42-43). Both the jet stream and the top of the cloud streak are at about 30,000 feet above the earth. From TIROS VII, June 23, 1963.

NASA

An Occluded Front (p. 93) from 700 miles up. This picture was taken at night by infrared scanners on NOAA 2, October 31, 1973. Pictures such as these help meteorologists fix the exact positions of storms and fronts over ocean areas (the storm center is off the New England coast). The infrared sensing permits meteorologists to determine the height of cloud tops. Note Florida peninsula in picture. Dark areas are warm; bright areas are cold.

Weather Maps

WEATHER MAPS summarize all the data sent to the central stations. Two kinds of maps are made: surface charts and upper air charts.

Surface charts plot the following for each station: wind direction and speed, pressure, temperature, dew point, visibility, current weather (rain, snow, fog, etc.), the amount and types of clouds and their heights, pressure changes in the past 3 hours, weather in the past 6 hours, and the amount and kind of precipitation. All this is shown by symbols in a space easily covered by a dime.

Once the data are plotted, the charts are analyzed by forecasting experts, who draw isobars to show lines of equal pressure. Then they mark the positions of fronts and show precipitation areas. From these analyzed charts, the forecasters prepare forecasts and weather bulletins. The methods of making forecasts are explained on pp. 134-146.

To understand forecasting methods, learn how to read the synoptic or general surface weather maps. Official National Weather Service maps are mailed weekly in an 8 page pamphlet which can be purchased for $7.50 a year from Superintendent of Documents, Washington, D.C. 20402. Newspaper weather maps are not so complete but give you data before you get the official maps by mail.

On this National Weather Service map, shaded areas show precipitation. Look for the isobars and for the fronts. Note the highs and lows and the symbols for air masses (mP over Washington and mT on the Texas Gulf). Symbols for station data are shown at the bottom of the page. On the backs of the Daily Weather Maps there appear, at intervals, a summary of weather symbols, analyses of unusual weather, and other general information.

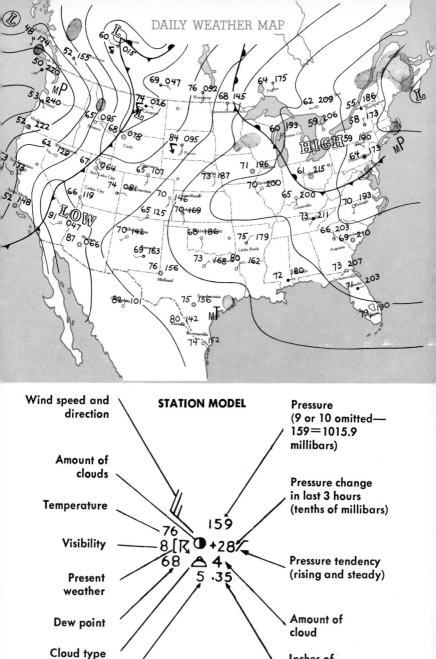

DAILY WEATHER MAP

STATION MODEL

Wind speed and direction

Amount of clouds

Temperature

Visibility

Present weather

Dew point

Cloud type

Height of cloud base

Pressure (9 or 10 omitted—159 = 1015.9 millibars)

Pressure change in last 3 hours (tenths of millibars)

Pressure tendency (rising and steady)

Amount of cloud

Inches of precipitation last 3 hours

76
8 [R   159
68   +28
    5 .35

133

FORECASTING FROM A SINGLE WEATHER MAP

is not difficult, although accuracy is limited to about 6 to 12 hours. Use good newspaper maps or National Weather Service daily maps. Short-range forecasts are based on the principle of persistence, which assumes, for example, that a front moving at 20 mph will continue at that rate with the same weather accompanying it, and that a stationary high will remain stationary. This principle is usually followed by expert forecasters. It generally works, though local conditions sometimes throw such predictions off.

Study the weather map below. For simplicity, only frontal positions are shown, with a precipitation area ahead of the warm front line. If you live at Dayton, Ohio, you know the cold front is 80 miles west, and moving at 20 mph. The front should pass Dayton in 4 hours. Your forecast? "Rain showers at about 2 p.m.—cooler tonight and tomorrow."

The making of a short-range forecast. It is now 10 AM; a cold front, still 80 miles from Dayton, is moving east at 20 mph. What is the forecast for Dayton?

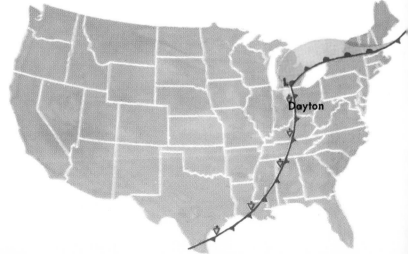

LIMITATIONS OF THE PERSISTENCE METHOD lie in the fact that many things can change a weather pattern. As the cold front (p. 134) approaches the Appalachians, portions may be slowed, air may be lifted slowly here and rapidly there, day and night will affect air-mass characteristics, and so forth. An experienced and trained forecaster can accurately estimate these things. A beginner cannot—so keep records and gain experience.

THE CONTINUITY METHOD OF FORECASTING is the persistence method with modifications. It can be used with fair accuracy for periods greater than 12 hours. You can make continuity forecasts by intelligent use of weather maps. The map below, and those on the next three pages, will show you the method. Monday's map, below, shows a wave centered in Colorado with a cold front extending southwest out of the low, and a warm front extending southeast. Rain showers lie along the cold front and a steady rain is falling ahead of the warm front. (See pp. 77-95 on fronts and their accompanying weather.)

Monday

COMPARISON OF DAILY WEATHER MAPS shows how fronts and the general weather pattern move and change. Compare Tuesday's map below with Monday's on the preceding page. The wave center has now moved to south central Nebraska, with the fronts extending out in much the same fashion as on Monday. But the warm sector of the wave (south of the wave center, or crest, connecting the two fronts) has become narrower. The area of precipitation ahead of the warm front sector has become much wider and, of course, the entire pattern has moved. Careful measurement, using the map scale at the bottom, shows that the crest of the wave has moved about 300 miles eastward.

Wednesday's map at the top of the next page shows that the low center has moved to northwestern Illinois. The cold air mass has overtaken the warm air mass and formed an occluded front (pp. 92-93) that extends from the low center to the southern tip of Illinois. Precipitation is much the same as before, except that steady rain now extends over the top of the occlusion.

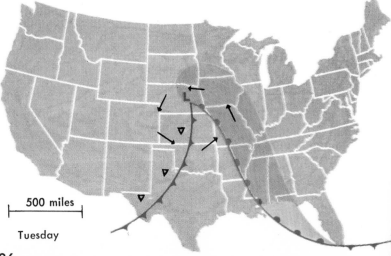

500 miles

Tuesday

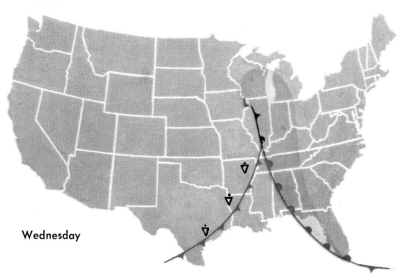

Wednesday

MAKE YOUR FORECAST by placing a blank map over the Monday, Tuesday, and Wednesday maps on the previous pages and tracing the frontal positions from them. Next draw arrows connecting the point of the wave for each day. Notice that the arrow connecting Tuesday and Wednesday points more northward than the first arrow connecting Monday and Tuesday positions.

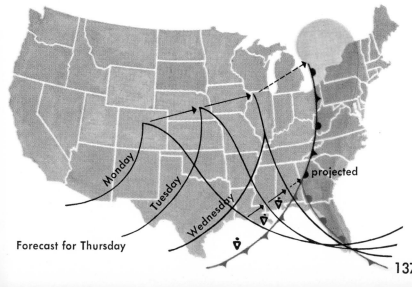

Monday

Tuesday

Wednesday

projected

Forecast for Thursday

To get the Thursday position of the tip of the occlusion, draw a dashed arrow pointing slightly more to the north but about the same length as the Tuesday-to-Wednesday arrow. The dashed arrow is to remind you that this is Wednesday and that you are making a forecast for Thursday. Now make arrows for the cold and warm fronts in the same way (refer to map at bottom of p. 137). Make sure the arrows for the fronts are perpendicular to the fronts. Next make broken forecast arrows for the fronts and draw your weather map for Thursday—on Wednesday. Be sure to draw in the precipitation belt the same as it was along the previous day's fronts.

The path of the point or crest of the wave on fronts (as on preceding maps) follows what is called a storm track. This is the path of bad weather. A knowledge of storm tracks will help you improve your forecasts. By fitting the path of the low crest from your forecast map to the storm track map below, a prediction for a period longer than 24 hours can be made.

If you systematically follow the weather maps and observe your local weather area, you should be able to make excellent short-range forecasts after a year or two of experience. A trained meteorologist, knowing the principles of local influences on weather, can make good local area forecasts within a week or so in a new area.

Storm tracks. The arrows show the paths which low cells generally follow over the United States. The tracks are more widely separated in winter than in summer.

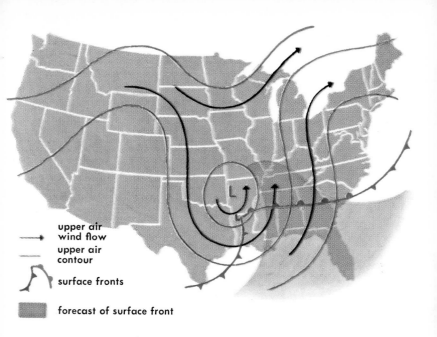

upper air
wind flow

upper air
contour

surface fronts

forecast of surface front

UPPER AIR PATTERNS AFFECT FORECASTS Although storms usually follow the storm tracks shown at the bottom of p. 138, they are sometimes thrown off by patterns of air flow in the upper air. The picture above shows how this happens. The green lines (contours) show the pressure pattern and the black arrows show wind direction of the upper air. Note the position of the upper air "closed low" cell—a complete low cell with the usual counterclockwise air rotation. It is high above the ground and is northwest of the surface low which lies at the crest of the wave formed at the frontal lines—conventionally shown in blue and red.

Were it not for the closed low cell in the air far above the earth, the surface low would probably follow the storm track marked A in the map at the bottom of p. 138. But the low-pressure center in the upper air "steers" the surface low north, resulting in the forecast pattern shown in purple, which represents the warm sector.

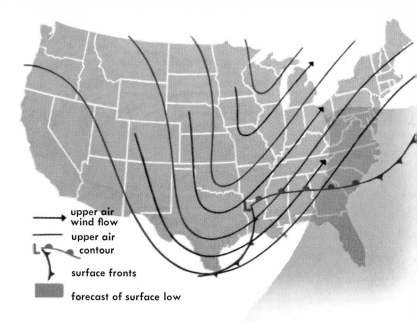

upper air
wind flow

upper air
contour

L surface fronts

forecast of surface low

THE MAP at the top of this page shows how differently a surface low will move if the upper air does not contain a closed low-pressure cell near it.

The surface situation is identical with that shown on the map on p. 139. But there is no closed low cell in the upper air pressure pattern shown by the green contours and black arrows. The air just above the surface low (marked in red at the tip of the frontal crest) is sweeping strongly to the northeast (wind in upper air follows contours—see p. 65). So the upper air will steer the surface low directly and rapidly to the northeast, resulting in the forecast pattern shown in purple. The low has moved a distance of 900 miles as compared to a movement of about 500 miles when the closed cell (p. 139) was present.

Upper air patterns are extremely important to accurate forecasting by the continuity method, but are not printed in newspapers. They are printed daily in the National Weather Service maps (see p. 141) and you should study them for most accurate forecasting.

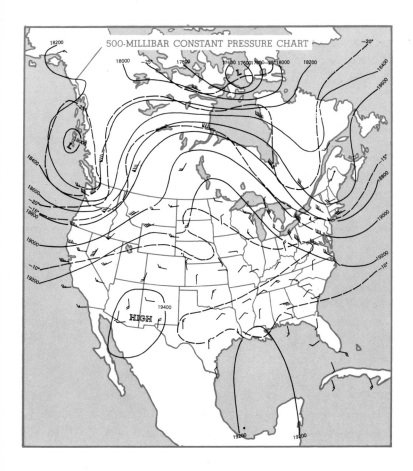

500-MILLIBAR CONSTANT PRESSURE CHART

CONSTANT PRESSURE MAPS of the upper air have contour lines showing altitude, not pressure. Solid lines show the height above sea level at which the air pressure is 500 millibars. The standard height of the 500-millibar level is 18,280 feet—but it can vary from 15,800 to 19,400 on a single chart. Note on this map that these heights are lowest in the north and highest in the south. Two upper air lows exist in the far north and northwest; a high lies over the Southwest. Dashed lines show centigrade temperature. Arrows show the wind.

MAKING YOUR OWN FORECASTS FROM OBSER-VATIONS Pages 112-141 explain how professional forecasters do their work and how you can do a reasonable job using good surface weather maps and upper air pressure charts—after a year or so of experience. It is possible to make fair-to-middling forecasts based on "weather signs," barometer, and weather-vane readings. If you use these things plus weather maps and a careful reading of the preceding sections of the book, you should be able to forecast your local weather with accuracy. However, it is the cooperative reports from hundreds of stations that make modern weather forecasts possible.

Most weather lore comes from farmers, hunters, and sailors—people most concerned with the weather. Many weather sayings have some truth in them—for wisdom accumulated as people gained experience, even before the reasons behind the facts were discovered. The saying "A ring around the moon means rain" is true 40 to 80 per cent of the time, depending on location, how the pressure is changing, the direction the clouds are moving, etc. If you use this rule modify it to: "If pressure is falling rapidly, a ring around the moon means rain in 18 to 48 hours, about 75 per cent of the time."

"A ring around the moon means rain"—sometimes!

WEATHER SIGNS have some prediction value if you know the atmospheric conditions they indicate. Here are the background facts for understanding what some weather signs mean. If you can explain these general rules-of-thumb in terms of more scientific meteorology, they will be of use to you.

It is interesting to collect local weather signs and lore. If you can talk with "old-timers" long resident in your region, see what they have to say. Then examine these beliefs in the light of present-day meteorology.

Weather will generally remain fair when:
The wind blows gently from west or northwest (p. 66).
Barometer remains steady or rises (pp. 85-88).
Cumulus clouds dot the summer sky in the afternoon (p. 20).
Morning fog breaks or "burns off" by noon (evidence of clear sky above).

Rainy weather or snow may come when:
Cirrus clouds thicken and are followed by lower clouds (p. 88). (Particularly true if barometer is dropping.)
There is a ring around the moon (pp. 17 & 88). (Particularly true if barometer is dropping.)
Puffy cumulus clouds begin to develop vertically (p. 20).
Sky is dark and threatening to the west (p. 85).
Southerly wind increases in speed with clouds moving from west (p. 85).
The wind—particularly a north wind—shifts in a counterclockwise direction—that is, from north to west to south (pp. 85-88).
The barometer falls steadily (pp. 85-88).

Weather will generally clear when:
Bases of clouds show steady rise to higher types (p. 85).
The wind—particularly an east wind—shifts to the west (p. 85).
The barometer rises rapidly (pp. 85 and 88).

Temperature will usually fall when:
Wind blows from—or shifts to—north or northwest (p. 85).
Night sky is clear and wind is light (pp. 9 and 14).
The barometer rises steadily in winter (p. 85).

Temperature will usually rise when:
Wind is from south, particularly with cloud cover at night or clear sky during the day (pp. 9 and 88).

A dependable, inexpensive aneroid barometer for home use.

Aneroid barometer combined with thermometer and humidity indicator.

A GOOD BAROMETER AND THIS TABLE (p. 145) will help you make reasonably good forecasts. The table is adapted from a National Weather Service table based on average conditions over the United States. Use the table in connection with good daily weather maps, and learn how conditions in your locality tend to vary (because of nearby mountains, lakes, ocean, or deserts, for example). A rapid rise or fall in barometric pressure (see second column in table) is 0.05 to 0.09 inches or more in 3 hours. A slow rise or fall is less than this. Barometric pressures in the table are in inches, adjusted to sea level. Calibrate your barometer to sea-level pressures by checking with your local weather station or airport. Every aneroid barometer has a device by which the pointer can be re-set. Once set to conform to a sea-level reading of an accurate barometer in your locality, it should require no further readjustment.

Be sure to keep records of your forecasts together with records of actual weather changes. Only in this way can you learn how local conditions affect the anticipated weather.

Wind Direction	Barometric Pressure	General Forecast
SW to NW	30.10 to 30.20—barometer steady	Fair, with little temperature change for 1 to 2 days
SW to NW	30.10 to 30.20—rising rapidly	Fair, with warmer weather and rain within 2 days
SW to NW	30.20 or above—barometer steady	Remaining fair with little temperature change
SW to NW	30.20 or above—falling slowly	Fair and slowly rising temperatures for about 2 days
S to SE	30.10 to 30.20—falling slowly	Rain within 24 hours
S to SE	30.10 to 30.20—falling rapidly	Rain within 12 to 24 hours. Wind will rise
SE to NE	30.10 to 30.20—falling slowly	Rain within 12 to 18 hours. Wind will rise
SE to NE	30 10 to 30.20—falling rapidly	Rain within 12 hours. Wind will rise
SE to NE	30.00 or below—falling slowly	Rain will continue 1 or more days
SE to NE	30.00 or below—falling rapidly	Rain with high winds in few hours. Clearing within 36 hours—colder in winter
E to NE	30.10 or above—falling slowly	Summer, with light winds: rain in 2 to 4 days. Winter, rain or snow within 24 hours
E to NE	30.10 or above—falling rapidly	Summer: probable rain in 12 to 24 hours. Winter: rain or snow within 12 hours
S to SW	30.00 or below—rising slowly	Clearing within a few hours. Then fair for several days
S to E	29.80 or below—falling rapidly	Severe storm within few hours. Then clearing within 24 hours—colder in winter
E to N	29.80 or below—falling rapidly	Severe storm (a "nor'easter" gale) in few hours. Heavy rains or snowstorm. Followed by cold wave in winter
Swinging to W	29.80 or below—rising rapidly	End of storm—clearing and colder

COMPUTER FORECASTING as accurate as human forecasting, or more so, is now being done by electronic computers. The U.S. Joint Numerical Weather Prediction Unit began operation of the first "electronic brain" for routine weather forecasting in 1955.

Computer forecasting is possible because movements of the atmosphere follow natural laws which can be expressed in mathematical equations. These equations are changed to coded instructions for the computer. Numerical figures, based on weather data, are fed into the computer. The electronic "brain" works out the predictions and prints forecast maps showing highs, lows, and other data.

Computer forecasting does not replace the meteorologist. Computers must be fed accurate data, and computer-produced maps must be interpreted and modified in terms of local conditions. But computer forecasting will save thousands of hours of routine work.

One of the early 36-hour forecast maps made by computer is shown below. Computer shades areas between contour lines and prints contour heights on grid points.

Weather and Climate

Climate is the weather at a given place over a period of time. It involves averages, totals, and extremes to set a picture of the weather pattern. Climate is affected by the same physical conditions that affect weather—latitude, prevailing winds, ocean currents, mountains, nearness to the sea, and the like. Climate might be called the generalized weather of an area.

Because climate, like weather, is made up of many factors, it is impossible to classify climates simply without ignoring some of them. Two places with the same range of temperature may have very different amounts of rainfall. Hence these two factors are more useful than either one alone. So climates are often classified by a combination of temperature (torrid, temperate, frigid) and rainfall (wet, humid, subhumid, semi-arid, arid). The most commonly used system stresses rainfall for the torrid and temperate zones, temperatures for the colder zones. This system (see map below) is useful because it corresponds to the natural vegetation of regions.

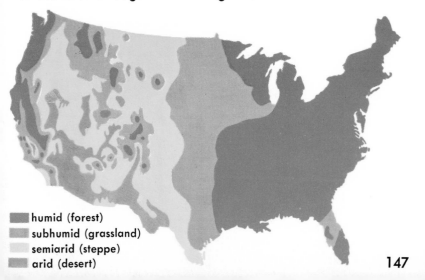

■ humid (forest)
■ subhumid (grassland)
■ semiarid (steppe)
■ arid (desert)

CLIMATIC DATA are important in agriculture and industry. Farmers need to know the length of growing seasons, extremes of temperature, average and minimum rainfall for successful growing of crops. The sale of air conditioners, sports clothes, and winter wear depends on seasonal temperature and rainfall. Many personal decisions involving painting, gardening, sports, trips, and vacations can be better made if climatic data are taken into account. The National Weather Service furnishes such information.

The climates of the United States vary considerably because of the size of the country and its varied terrain. National Weather Service figures, recorded since 1899, give a full picture of the temperature, humidity, precipitation, sunshine, frosts, storms, and other climatic factors. These data are presented on maps for easy reference. The most important of such data appear on the following maps.

AVERAGE TEMPERATURE is the most commonly used climate statistic. It is of limited use and is of more value when used with the next two maps.

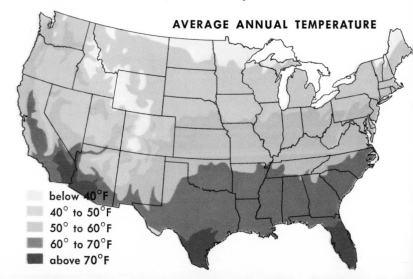

AVERAGE ANNUAL TEMPERATURE

- below 40°F
- 40° to 50°F
- 50° to 60°F
- 60° to 70°F
- above 70°F

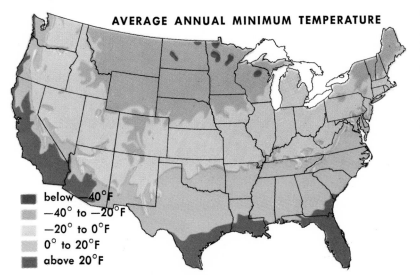

AVERAGE ANNUAL MINIMUM TEMPERATURE

- below −40°F
- −40° to −20°F
- −20° to 0°F
- 0° to 20°F
- above 20°F

AVERAGE LOWEST TEMPERATURE is more important to people like farmers and fruit growers than average annual temperatures. Map above shows this.

AVERAGE TEMPERATURE OF HOT MONTHS helps in deciding where to live, in what kind of house, what plants to grow, or if air conditioning is needed.

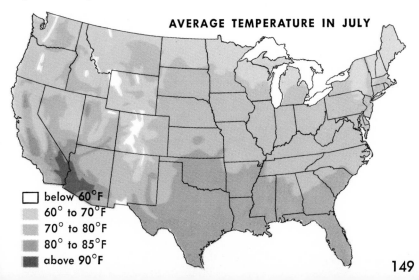

AVERAGE TEMPERATURE IN JULY

- below 60°F
- 60° to 70°F
- 70° to 80°F
- 80° to 85°F
- above 90°F

149

AVERAGE ANNUAL PRECIPITATION IN INCHES

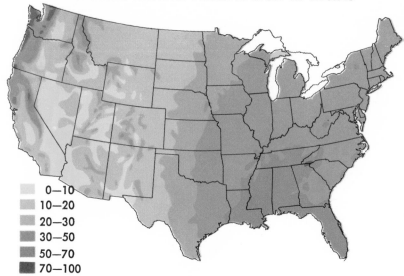

0—10
10—20
20—30
30—50
50—70
70—100

AVERAGE PRECIPITATION—mainly rain and snow—is important to determine types of crops that can be grown.

LACK OF RAINFALL ruins farmers. Twenty inches is minimum for most crops.

PER CENT OF YEARS WITH LESS THAN 20 INCHES OF PRECIPITATION

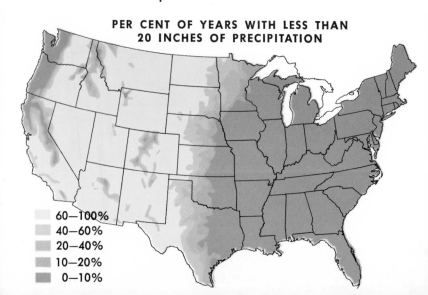

60—100%
40—60%
20—40%
10—20%
0—10%

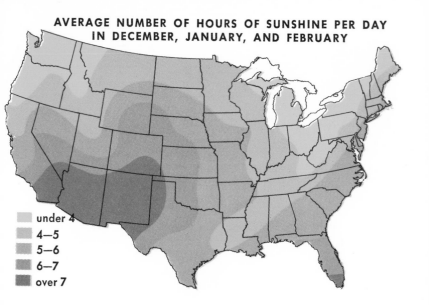

AVERAGE NUMBER OF HOURS OF SUNSHINE PER DAY IN DECEMBER, JANUARY, AND FEBRUARY

under 4
4—5
5—6
6—7
over 7

WINTER SUNSHINE makes Florida, California, and the Southwest famous. It is important, too, for agriculture.

NUMBER OF CLEAR DAYS is different from average daily sunshine. Note southern Florida and California.

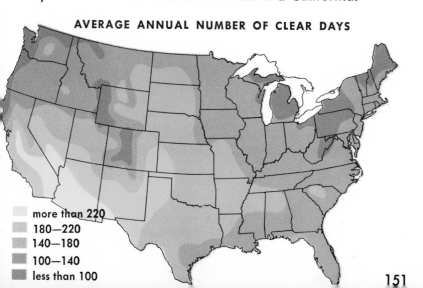

AVERAGE ANNUAL NUMBER OF CLEAR DAYS

more than 220
180—220
140—180
100—140
less than 100

151

AVERAGE RELATIVE HUMIDITY IN JULY
AT NOON, LOCAL TIME

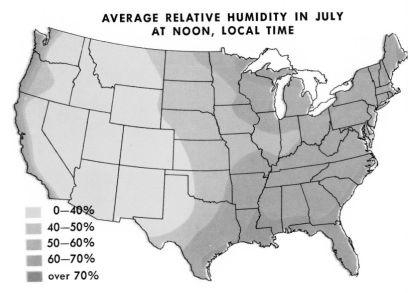

0—40%
40—50%
50—60%
60—70%
over 70%

RELATIVE HUMIDITY spells comfort or discomfort. Summer humidity is high in coastal areas.

NUMBER OF DAYS WITH SNOW ON GROUND is of interest to skiers and farmers. Snow means spring water.

AVERAGE ANNUAL NUMBER OF DAYS WITH SNOW COVER
(1 INCH OR MORE)

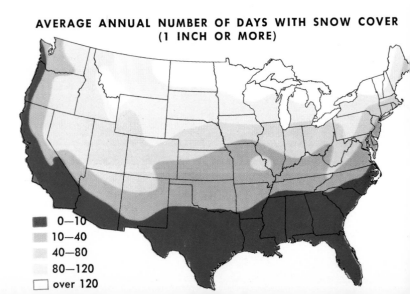

0—10
10—40
40—80
80—120
over 120

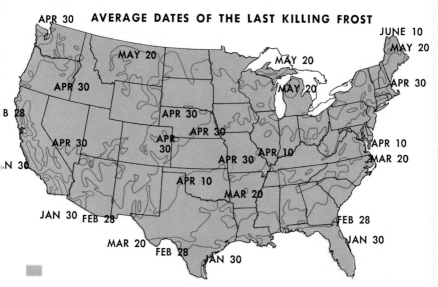

AVERAGE DATES OF THE LAST KILLING FROST

APR 30

JUNE 10
MAY 20

MAY 20

MAY 20

APR 30

MAY 20

APR 30

APR 30

APR 30

APR 30

APR 30

APR 10

APR 10

APR 10

APR 10

MAR 20

MAR 20

B 28

N 30

JAN 30 FEB 28

MAR 20 FEB 28 JAN 30

FEB 28

JAN 30

WHEN CAN YOU SAFELY PLANT YOUR GARDEN?

Map shows dates of last killing frosts in spring.

THE GROWING SEASON determines what plants can be grown and the number of crops per season.

AVERAGE LENGTH OF THE FROST-FREE PERIOD IN DAYS

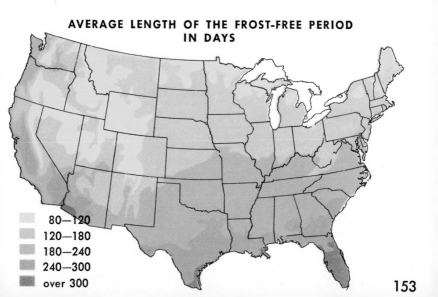

- 80—120
- 120—180
- 180—240
- 240—300
- over 300

153

MICROCLIMATES Geographical, biological, and man-made factors often make local climatic conditions different from the general climate. A local climatic pattern is called a microclimate. Large inland lakes moderate temperature extremes. The result is climatic differences between the windward and lee sides—for example, between Milwaukee, on windward side of Lake Michigan, and Grand Haven, on the lee side, only 85 miles east (see first table below).

Plants create microclimatic differences chiefly by their use of water and by their effect on winds (see second table below). Windbreaks are grown to make a favorable

MICROCLIMATIC DIFFERENCES BETWEEN LAKESIDE CITIES

Climatic condition	Period of year	Milwaukee windward shore	Grand Haven leeward shore
Av. temp.	January		3.6°F higher
Av. temp.	August	2.0°F higher	
Precipitation	Dec.-Feb.		2.09 in. more
Precipitation	June-Aug.	0.55 in. more	
Snowfall	Jan.-Dec.		44 days more
Rel. humidity	Dec.-Feb.		5% more
Wind speed	Dec.-Feb.		1.4 mph more

BETWEEN FORESTS AND OPEN LAND

Forests	Open land
Warmer in winter	Warmer in summer
Wind speeds reduced	Wind speeds higher
Relative humidity higher	Relative humidity lower
Water storage high	Water storage low

microclimate on farms. The placement of a new dwelling in regard to frost drainage, local breezes, and utilization of winter sunlight may make great difference in livability, and in fuel economy during winter.

Heavy, cold air flows downhill, forming cold pockets in valleys. Frost is much more common there; so oranges, grapes, and apples are planted on hillsides to insure "frost drainage" when cold spells come. The first table below shows microclimatic differences between valleys and hills.

Cities induce convection currents which cause higher clouds and somewhat more rain than in the nearby country. Because of sewer drainage in cities, less water stands and evaporates. Thus relative humidity is lower in cities. The second chart below shows other differences.

MICROCLIMATIC DIFFERENCES BETWEEN VALLEYS AND HILLS

Climatic condition	Period	Valleys	Hills
Minimum temp.	daily	much lower	higher
Temp. range	daily & annual	larger	smaller
Frost	night	more	less
Wind speed	night	lower	higher
Fog	morning	more	less

BETWEEN CITY AND COUNTRYSIDE

City	Countryside
Haze and smog	Clear
Temperature higher	Temperature lower
Wind speed and radiation less	Wind speed and radiation higher

IS OUR CLIMATE CHANGING? Recent newspaper and magazine articles have claimed that our climate is warming up. Perhaps this is true—perhaps not.

Through geological history the normal climate of the earth was so warm that subtropical weather reached to 60°N and S and there was a total absence of polar ice.

It is only during less than 1 per cent of the earth's history that glaciers have reached down from the polar areas to what is now the temperate zone of the northern hemisphere. The latest such advance, which started about 1,000,000 years ago, was marked by geological upheaval and the beginning of man. During this time vast ice sheets advanced and retreated over the continents, the last retreat occurring 30,000 to 40,000 years ago.

Within recorded history there have been minor glacial advances and retreats. Alpine passes now covered with ice were used from A.D. 600 to 700. Ships sailed from Leif Ericson's Greenland through routes now blocked by ice floes. From A.D. 1000 to 1200 there were flourishing settlements in Greenland. Gradually, cooling of the climate forced their abandonment about the year 1400.

Is the earth really warming? A 2°F increase in the earth's overall temperature would clear the polar seas of all ice. Yet today in parts of western North America glaciers are perceptibly advancing while the east coast seems to be warming.

We have routine temperature measurements for only 100 years—and these not too reliable, because of changes in instruments and methods of observation.

The only conclusion to be drawn about our climate is that we do not know whether it is changing drastically. Geologically we may be at the end of the Ice Age, or we may just be having a breathing spell of a few centuries before the next advance of the glaciers.

BOOKS FOR MORE INFORMATION

The following books will further your knowledge and enjoyment of weather. The National Weather Service, Washington, D.C., publishes monographs and periodicals on all phases of meteorology. Write for a free list of government weather publications to the Superintendent of Documents, Washington, D.C. 20402.

Battan, Louis J., THE UNCLEAN SKY, Anchor Books, Doubleday & Co., Garden City, N.Y. 1969. A description of air pollution and its effects in easily understandable terms.

Byers, Horace Robert, GENERAL METEOROLOGY, McGraw-Hill Book Co., New York, 1959. An introductory college text covering basic principles.

Cantzlaar, George L., YOUR GUIDE TO THE WEATHER, Barnes and Noble, New York, 1964. A simple, interesting, non-technical account of the weather. Accurate diagrams aid to understanding.

Cole, Franklyn W., INTRODUCTION TO METEOROLOGY, John Wiley & Sons, New York, 1970. An introduction to Meteorological science for the non-scientist.

Critchfield, Howard J., GENERAL CLIMATOLOGY, Prentice Hall, New Jersey, 1966 (2nd edition). A basic text covering regional, physical and applied climatology.

Laird, Charles and Ruth, WEATHERCASTING. A HANDBOOK OF AMATEUR METEOROLOGY. Prentice-Hall, Englewood Cliffs, N.J., 1955. Explains basic principles of observing, forecasting, and construction of weather instruments for the amateur.

Trewartha, Glenn T., THE EARTH'S PROBLEM CLIMATES, Univ. of Wisconsin Press, Madison, 1961. A survey of the characteristics and causes of problem climates of the earth.

PERIODICALS

WEATHERWISE, American Meteorological Society, 45 Beacon Street, Boston 8, Mass. Non-technical, bi-monthly weather magazine containing surveys and many "how to" articles. February issue each year is an almanac of previous year's weather.

AVERAGE MONTHLY WEATHER OUTLOOK, National Weather Service (order from Superintendent of Documents). Graphic presentation of preceding month's weather and estimate of expected rainfall and temperatures for next 30 days. Issued twice monthly.

INDEX

Asterisks (*) indicate illustrations.

MEASURING SCALE (IN MILLIMETERS AND CENTIMETERS)

1 2 3 4 5 6 7 8 9 10 11 12 13

MEASURING SCALE (IN TENTHS OF AN INCH)

K   L